A Parents' Guide:

RELIGION

FOR LITTLE CHILDREN

A Parents' Guide:

RELIGION
for Little Children

**Including an Appendix of The 76 Most Asked Questions
and Their Answers**

by CHRISTIANE BRUSSELMANS
with EDWARD WAKIN

from
the little art shop
of the Benedictine
monastery of
Regina Laudis
Bethlehem, conn.

OUR SUNDAY VISITOR, INC.
Huntington, Indiana 46750

Nihil Obstat: Rev. Lawrence Gollner, Censor Librorum

Imprimatur: ✠Leo A. Pursley, D.D. Bishop of Fort Wayne-
South Bend

Photo Credits: Edward Lettau, pages 14, 16, 32, 34, 39, 41, 43,
45, 51, 57, 61, 63, 65, 67, 73, 75, 78, 81, 86, 88, 92, 97,
115, 123, 129, 135, 139. Jean Fortier, pages 26, 36, 49, 53,
55, 83, 90, 94, 95, 111, 121, 137. World Wide, page 127.

Quotations from "Good News for Modern Man,"
the New Testament in Today's English Version,
copyright American Bible Society, New York 1966.

The text and music of the antiphons are taken from:
L. DEISS, "BIBLICAL HYMNS AND PSALMS, volume I,
© World Library Publications, Inc. 2145 Central Parkway,
Cincinnati, Ohio, 45214. All rights reserved

ISBN: 0-87973-825-1

Library of Congress Card No. 76-140110

Sixth Printing, 1975

Published, printed and bound in the U.S.A by
OUR SUNDAY VISITOR, INC.
Noll Plaza, Huntington, Indiana   46750

Contents

FOREWORD

AT the end of World War II, one of the leading catechists in the Western world was a little girl sitting on the porch of a large Belgian house, uttering her first words in English. She was singing "Swing Low, Sweet Chariot" with Negro GI's. Soon after, she had learned a string of Negro spirituals, which she recalls as the beginning of her biblical training.

The GI's were running the kitchen for the military headquarters set up in her family home after the D-Day invasion of Europe. The 13-year-old girl was one of ten children of a prominent law professor caught up in the fortunes of war.

The girl, who is still singing the praises of the Lord, is appropriately a celebrated religious educator in the United States as well as Belgium, a trans-Atlantic phenomenon in the field of religious education. Her first instructors in English and in the Bible would hardly recognize the little Belgian girl as Dr. Christiane Brusselmans of the faculties of Louvain and Fordham, author, lecturer, teacher, and authority in catechetics.

See how she runs: A professor in pastoral catechetics in the Theology Department of the Catholic University of Louvain during the fall; a professor in religious education at the Graduate Institute for Religious Education at Fordham University in the spring; a lecturer throughout the northeastern and midwestern United States before conventions, parents' groups, and Confraternity of Christian Doctrine educators; a consultant and field work director in Harlem and mid-town New York City; author of articles for both scholarly and popular magazines, encyclopedias, and academic journals as well as practical books for parents.

Dr. Brusselmans' latest honor is the Pius X Award presented by Terence Cardinal Cooke and the New York Archdiocesan CCD Office. It placed a seal of recognition on what parents, religious educators, CCD directors, students, and colleagues say about her: "dynamic" . . . "her great appeal is that she doesn't talk in generalities; she makes religion teaching come alive" . . . "she puts everything in the concrete" . . . "when Christiane demonstrates ways to teach religion, it all comes alive as she sings, laughs, uses examples that make sense to the children—and in all this, her theology is always sound."

A sampling of the demand for her appearances is reflected in a month's activity in the United States: Featured speaker at the New England CCD Congress in Providence, R.I., then to Buffalo, New York, where she played the leading role in a Workshop in Pastoral Catechetics.

Appearances in Milwaukee and Chicago, then back to Paterson, New Jersey, for a diocesan-wide meeting of priests in the afternoon and parents in the evening—followed by the CCD Congress of the Paterson Diocese. Add Boston and New York for video-taping; then back to Belgium in time for the beginning of the fall term at Louvain, then the spring term at Fordham, more lectures, appearances, writing, etc.

But if the pace sounds hectic on paper, the style of Christiane Brusselmans is not. She is warm, attentive, lively, laughing, apt to sing a song to make a point, inclined to slap her forehead to express surprise. One thing she is not, and that is lethargic.

In all this, she has a basic message in her method: "Parents be what you are, and being what you are you will bring

Christ to your child. Your love, affection, security, care will do it."

Or as she puts it with italicized emphasis in this book on religion for pre-schoolers: "*Christian witness is the most important contribution of parents to the religious education of their children.*"

This book, which appeared in abridged form in *Our Sunday Visitor*, produced an unusual outpouring of mail from grateful parents who, in effect, thanked her for "telling it like it is," for confronting the responsibility for religious education in warm and informed terms, in practical and realistic ways.

Religion for Little Children: A Parents' Guide—carries the full force of her expertise, her skill and her enriched first-hand experience.

In the book, she develops her dominant theme: the home is the "most important classroom for religious education." The full implications are spelled out in keeping with the Brusselmans approach toward religious education.

The book begins with the mother-to-be, discussing how Baptism can become meaningful for the whole family and tracing the child's religious development from the cradle to the classroom. The specific topics include the early development of faith surrounded by parental love and parallel the child's physical and psychological development by exploring the ways religion is communicated in a visual way, a verbal way and then in a written way.

All discoveries that the child makes of life around him in the home and in church are described in ways that will help the parent draw out the religious capacities of the growing child. There are special sections on the holydays and holy seasons of the year as well as useful commentary for all members of the family ranging from brothers and sisters to grandparents.

Throughout the book, however, the focus is on parents' response to the religious needs of children. An extensive, practical question-and-answer section is included to provide parents with specific information on how to respond to the almost infinite number of religiously-related questions little children ask.

Dr. Brusselmans faces these questions right in her own family. She has 38 nephews and nieces! They, in fact, are the reason she became involved in religious education in the first place.

It started while she was studying for her bachelor's and master's degrees in theology from 1955 to 1960 at Louvain under an illustrious faculty which included Edward Schillebeeckx, Francois Houtart and Charles Moeller. That theological period came after a very practical period: Work as a nurse's assistant, two years as a wandering folk singer in Europe, a short period as a poultry farmer (selling 200 chickens a week) on the family estate to pay the bills while her father recovered from an illness.

While she was at Louvain, her brothers and sisters— then mothers and fathers—complained to her about the poor quality of religious education being served up to their children. So at their urging, Christiane opened a Sunday school for her own family's children.

After finishing Louvain, she went in search of more know-how in religious education. This brought her to the renowned Institut Catholique in Paris, where she studied and did field work with a variety of children, from brain-damaged and disadvantaged children to suburban children and children brought up by Communist parents in Paris' "Red Belt."

Before she had finished her Paris studies, Americans once again came into her life. This time it was an American Jesuit and a layman doing research in philosophy. They urged her to continue her work in the U.S. and, in fact, filled out an application for her at Catholic University. With her characteristic aplomb, she signed and mailed it.

The next thing she knew, she was offered an instructor's position, an early and quick recognition of her abilities. So she landed in the United States for the first time as a teacher of future teachers of catechetics. Besides teaching, she earned a doctorate in religious education from Catholic University.

From there, it was soon Louvain, Fordham, two books that have sold over 100,000 copies (*I Go to Mass with God's Family* and *I Receive God's Peace*) and the inevitable development of a Brusselmans' American following wherever parents are concerned about religious education of children.

Her approach encompasses the three pillars of religious development for the child—the family, the school and the parish's liturgical life. Collaboration and involvement characterize an approach in which the parent helps to teach his child, even in the religious school, and both join in liturgical activities.

For Christiane Brusselmans, the fall of 1969 and the spring of 1970 constituted the year of the parent. She stressed lectures, meetings and talks with parents on religious education. All this culminated in the completion of this religious guide for parents of pre-school children.

Next, it became the year of the clergy for Christiane Brusselmans. She is directing more and more of her attention to working with bishops and priests as part of the Brusselmans' formula for joining all helping hands in the catechetical task of teaching the Faith.—*Edward Wakin*

INTRODUCTION

*F*ROM the moment of birth, religious education begins for the children of God. It is good psychology as well as theology. Psychologists have impressively established the fact that the child is father of the man. From that first marvelous moment of life, learning begins at an incredible speed; by the age of six, the child has made tremendous strides in physical, psychological and spiritual growth.

It is in the crib that the awakening and growth of faith must begin, in the child's room, in his home, in the yard, in his neighborhood, among his young friends, and among the adult people who surround him in a tight little circle of love. The Christian educational mission for a parent starts in the concrete here and now.

Parents obviously do not wait until their children enter the first grade to teach them how to walk, how to eat, how to speak, how to relate and play with others. Nor should they wait until the child is six to help him discover God's love through their own love, through wonder and praise of the Lord for all the new things which a child discovers in the world. A child can and should discover the world with a view which reaches beyond the human. He can perceive a Christian meaning and dimension of life if careful and conscientious Christian parents help him see beyond human signs to the revelation of God and His love for man and mankind. The parent can guide the child to see God's gifts in people and things, and then relate them to Him who is the source of all love, of all creativity, of all beauty, of all life.

For the Christian parent there is a great reward in all this. A young child can be a means to true sacramental grace for his parents and in the process parents will rediscover their own Christian vision of life. Happy is the child who has received faith in Christ through his parents, and happy are those parents who through their children have renewed their faith and commitment to Christ.

From my own family experience—a family of ten brothers and sisters and thirty-eight nephews and nieces—the paramount role of the family in the growth of faith of the child has been borne out. Mature Christian faith, attitudes, values and commitment in the world are received in and through a Christian family.

"I am loved. Some day I will love in return..."

It is through parent-child relationship and interaction that an individual's religious values and attitudes are developed in early years. The child identifies with his parents by adopting their attitudes, their values and their vision of life—both explicitly stated and implicitly contained in their approach towards life.

My point is this: religious education should be returned to where it belongs, to the family. It is from the family that it will extend and expand. From this strong base, as the world of the child extends to the Christian community, to school, parish, neighborhood, and nation, our children will be able to mature into adult Christians. They can then really enter into a Christian commitment to God and their fellow men.

This doesn't mean that parochial schools and CCD programs have no role, no mission in helping the parents reach this goal for their children. But their role is complementary to the role of the family; their influence is secondary. Parents must realize that they should not wait until their child enters first grade or starts his religion classes to help him achieve creative growth in the life of faith, love, and hope—the gifts received on the day of baptism in the faith of the Church.

The importance of the family is brought home by discouraging experiences with the very limited success of Catholic schools and CCD programs in forming mature Christians. This partial failure of schools is related to the crisis of faith and the challenges facing Christians in an increasingly changing and secular world. What is needed is parent education and a re-evaluation of the widespread tendency of parents to give up their responsibility for being the religious educators of their children. Many have delayed until the first-grader is taken into CCD classes or into Catholic schools. There they expect the Sisters and teachers to work miracles.

To achieve successful religious education, Catholic and CCD schools must enlist and enlighten Christian parents. Adult education for parents-to-be and for existing parents

Religious education should be returned to where it belongs...

on the religious development of their children and the paramount importance of pre-school years should greatly improve the effectiveness of formal religious education in later years. When basic Christian attitudes and values have been developed in early childhood, formal education can reinforce through a more cognitive approach the pre-existing Christian attitudes and values received in the family.

Thus, this book is concerned with the religious education which parents can and should give their very young children. Beyond parents and grandparents to whom this book is directed, we also address ourselves to priests, parish religious coordinators, and nursery school teachers who help parents carry on their mission and responsibility. We all must face the fact that early childhood is crucial for Christian experiences and the formation of Christian attitudes and values that will shape future religious development of the child.

The religious education of young children is an awesome subject to tackle, but its very importance—also neglect —calls for a conscientious and thorough set of answers to the religious questions children ask and the questions parents ask about the religious care and feeding of their children.

Chapter 1

Preparing for Baptism

WITH each birth something extraordinary, something special occurs in the life of the Christian family. It is not something to stumble into spiritually, any more than it is stumbled into medically and psychologically. Christian parents exchanging information and experiences should move forward together to meet the experience of a child being born.

The time to begin preparing for Baptism is when a couple knows that another Christian is going to be born. The guidance doctors and psychologists have given prospective parents on the physical and emotional levels must also be given on the religious level.

Unfortunately, the spiritual preparation of Christian parents for the baptism of their child has been largely nonexistent in our parishes. Pastors must be reminded of this need to provide pastoral orientation and guidance for Christian parents. For when parents bring a child to birth, they bring a disciple of Christ to birth, too. Through Christian parents, the substance of humanity in the baptismal transformation turns into the substance of the Body of Christ.

Pastors and those who assist them should offer parents-to-be an educational program centered around the baptismal event. Through such a program, parents would understand more deeply the important decision they make for their children when seeking Baptism for them.

The parish is the logical place to start such a program. A group of couples who are expecting babies can be brought together. A parish announcement or invitations from the pastor will do it. The group—husbands and wives —can meet and talk freely about the responsibility and the challenges of Christian parenthood.

At least a month before Baptism, parents should register with the parish church and a regular educational program should begin. This could take place in the homes of the parents-to-be on a rotating basis or in the parish center. Personally, I prefer the informal setting of the home where parents can share their experiences and thoughts with greater ease. Awareness of Christian parenthood is increased in conversations with different people in the same phase of the same experience. They share their own insights, and they can also be stimulated by Christian parents who have already gone through the process and who volunteer their services as resource people. Such programs could take place several times during the year as new couples come along. These groups also can start implementing what the renewed Rite of Infant Baptism calls for—a solemn communal celebration of Baptism.

The last pre-baptismal meeting could be given over to preparation for baptismal celebration during a Sunday Mass in the presence of a large segment of the parish community. In my parish such celebrations takes place every First Sunday of the month at the 5 p.m. Mass. One can immediately sense how meaningful such as sacramental celebration becomes for those parents, godparents and other family members who have prepared several weeks for this life-giving event.

The preparatory meetings will bring up many questions Christian parents have often asked themselves or it will be the opportunity to face important questions that never occurred to them. The basic question that should be raised is: "Why are you having your child baptized?"

An analysis of the answers given to this question reveals

that both practicing and non-practicing Christian parents see in Baptism a response to the vital needs of man in a variety of ways.

First, there is the need for the child to belong to a determined sociological group. In such a case, Baptism allows the child to participate in the socio-cultural group in which he is born. It becomes not so much a matter of making the child a member of the Church than a matter of making him a certified member of the socio-cultural group to which his parents belong. Such motivation can best be described as post-Christian tribal paganism.

Also, along with this need and often connected with it, the baptism of a child fulfills the human desire of providing an opportunity to celebrate the perfectly understandable human joy at the birth of a child. In this case, infant baptism appears as a rite of natural religion, as the means of entering into life and into the security of a group.

Another human need to which Baptism provides an answer is the desire of parents to obtain security for their children, and, especially, to assure them of an eternal life insurance against the annihilation of death. In such a view, Baptism opens a savings account for their children. New deposits will be made by bringing the children to the other sacraments of the Church, so that one day they will enjoy eternal retirement.

Finally, we find those Christian parents who in full understanding of Baptism seek the life of the Church, expressed in faith in Jesus Christ. What they ask for is faith—faith in the life, the death, the resurrection and the second coming of the Lord; what they promise is to help their children identify with Christ and the message of the Gospel through daily faithfulness to their baptismal commitment.

Thus, an analysis of the motivations of parents asking baptism for their children shows a great variety of answers and values. In some cases, mere ignorance; in others, sociological, even magical, understanding of the sacrament. However, what is common to all these human motivations is the deep and loving care parents have for their children. There should be no question of simply dismissing or condemning these human motivations. They serve as stepping stones to a further awareness and a serious religious inquiry into the faith which the Church gives to a person through Baptism, the sacrament of faith. The human motivations reveal, in fact, a "sense of the sacred," a feeling for the religious. They reflect concern for the "beyond," and seek the intervention of some supernatural power—someone who can guarantee eternal survival and happiness to their child.

Undoubtedly, we have here human and religious values which are inscribed in the deepest recesses of the human heart. But, even if there is a certain sense of God, often there is no clear and explicit reference to faith in the resurrection of Jesus Christ. What baptismal educational programs should offer to such parents is the chance to grow from religious beliefs without faith into a Christian faith founded on Jesus Christ.

Parents are ready, motivated and willing, to grow in their faith. Will there be someone in the person of the pastor or his collaborators to answer their need?

Another, more specific question that is frequently asked at parent-meetings is "What about the Church's teaching: Outside the Church no salvation?" or in other words: "Without Baptism no salvation? What about limbo? What about children dying without Baptism in the Church?"

Such questions enter deep theological territory and parish groups can be well-served by a competent theologian explaining the answers in person. For our purposes, the following will help to clarify the problem:

Although God's universal plan of salvation wills a sharing of His divine life with all men, at the same time it should be remembered that it is in and through Jesus Christ that all past, present and future generations are redeemed. Vatican Council II reiterates this traditional and central teaching on the necessity of the Church for Salvation in *Lumen Gentium* (Chap. II:14): "For Christ, made present to us in His body, which is the Church, is the one Mediator and the unique Way of salvation. He Himself affirmed the necessity of faith and Baptism (Mt. 16: 16; Jn. 3:5). Whoever therefore, knowing that the Catholic Church was made necessary by God through Jesus Christ, would refuse to enter her or to remain in her could not be saved.

However, a growing number of Christian parents, who have a deep reverence for the sacrament of Baptism and concern for the baptismal commitment which they accept for their child, question the actual practice of infant baptism. They ask: "Would it not be preferable to postpone baptism until our children are mature enough to make a free choice on whether or not to be baptized?" These parents are concerned lest they violate the freedom of their children by having them baptized as infants when they cannot make up their own minds. The problem has been given added urgency by adolescents who complain, "Why did our parents make us members of the Catholic Church? We were never asked, and here we are, stuck in it, when we want to get out."

Let's first try to answer this last question, which seems more theoretical than practical, from a human point of view.

A person really can't say, "I am without father and mother" or "I stand alone, by myself. I am without a history." Whatever he does or says, he must accept his heritage—the many-faceted physical, psychological, cultural, spiritual and financial heritage of his parents. A child does not wait until eighteen to select his nationality, his culture, or the language he will learn. Parents very logically and realistically realize that they are not going to wait until their children are eighteen to give them a certain home environment which creates attitudes and values in order to help them to grow into healthy personalities.

Here is what needs to be said to Christian parents: "If you have one value in your life, it is the faith that you are risen in the Lord. You share in Christian hope and faith, and try to live Christ's love in this world, starting in your own family. Do you think that it is reasonable to deprive your child of this heritage until he is able to make a mature decision? Even if you don't have him baptized, will you be so completely neutral in your home so as to leave his choice completely free on whether or not he would be baptized?" Yet to answer this legitimate question adequately it is necessary to seek the Church's point of view, which in turn demands that we cite the history of infant baptism.

The tradition and the practice of infant baptism has been under examination during the past 20 years in the Protestant churches. One of their best theologians, Professor J. Jeremias, made a careful study of infant baptism during the first centuries of the Church. He affirms that the Church has always practiced the baptism of infants, with the exception of one crisis that arose in the fourth century and which extended only to a small portion of Christian parents.

Thus, infant baptism has always been practiced in the entire church and this tradition has continued to our own time. It was Saint Augustine who first justified this practice from a theological point of view. For Saint Augustine there exists no doubt about the necessity of baptizing newly born infants. The rule is simple: All Christian parents must present their children for Baptism. This practice is rooted in the doctrine that Baptism is rightly called the Sacrament of Faith, because the adherence of the believer to the faith of the Church is a constitutive element of the sacrament.

As a result, Saint Augustine justifies infant baptism by distinguishing the ways in which a child can be said to receive and profess the Faith of the Church. Augustine first mentions the faith of the child itself. As clearly expressed in the new Rite of Infant Baptism, baptism requires a profession of faith on the part of the one to be baptized. In the case of an infant, this profession of faith is made by the parents. Through this ritualistic act, the parents present their child to receive the Faith of the Church and in his name promise to adhere to it. This solemn profession makes the child a believer in virtue of the efficacity of the sacrament, based on the will of Christ to save the believer and on the family solidarity which leads parents to have their child incorporated in Christ. If, psychologically, the child

remains unchanged, he is nevertheless transformed onto-
logically into a Christian. As the child grows, it will primarily
be the responsibility of the Christian parents to have it
progressively discover and personally adhere to the Faith of
the Church. Saint Augustine, with his remarkable pastoral
realism, does not exclude the possibility of discovering in
some parents a faith that is at best defective, if it exists at
all. It is here that he introduces a new dimension to the faith
of both child and parents which is the Faith of the Church.

During the sacramental celebration, the parents surrounded by the Christian community are the visible sign of
the Faith of the Church. It is, therefore, most fitting that
we find the following dialogue in the baptismal rite:

"What do you ask of God's Church for N . . . ?"

"Faith."

Baptism is a communal work and it should be of the
greatest concern for the whole faith. It is the entire parish
community which welcomes the newly-born infants and
communicates its faith to them. It is the entire Christian
community which binds itself as the guarantor of the faith
of the children that it has welcomed and baptized to a new
life.

Hopefully, more and more parishes will solemnly celebrate the baptism of its new members in the presence of a
substantial number of parishioners. In doing so, Christian
communities will more fully realize their corporate responsibility in transmitting the faith. Thus, we are all vitally concerned in the entrance of new members into the family of
God.

Parents preparing for the baptism of their infants will
greatly benefit by careful study of the new ritual of infant
baptism. Children and other family members might join in
by preparing the songs and readings that will enhance celebration of the sacrament.

Chapter 2

The Encounter: Baptism

*I*N the new rite of infant baptism we find another option for the welcoming dialogue which is as follows:

"What do you ask of God's Church for N. . . .?"

"Faith."

When parents bring their child for Baptism, the infant receives a new life which is God's own divine life and love. The life of a baptized infant therefore acquires a new meaning and a new dignity. Through Christ he becomes son of God and brother of all men. Through Christ he receives salvation.

Officially, the infant has been accepted and given the faith of the Christian community. Henceforth, the Church will be there to help this child grow towards mature faith and Christian commitment in the world. In the new rite, the church officially entrusts to the child's parents and family the responsibility for growth of a faith that is a seed to be cultivated. As the child matures, other members of the community—such as sponsors, catechists, leaders of youth movements and the clergy—will help Christian parents carry on their duties.

Infant baptism only realizes its full meaning if Christian parents are willing to fulfill the mission which they received from the Church for their children. The baptism of a young child is not so much a matter of having baptismal water poured on the infant's forehead while the minister pronounces the sacramental words; "I baptize you in the name of the Father, of the Son, and of the Holy Spirit." Baptism is not only a matter of sacramental words, objects, and gestures. The sacrament is much more than that. It is a personal encounter between Christ and the believer; it is the Sacrament of Faith. If, on one hand, Christ is willing to share his life with the person, on the other hand that person must be willing through his "Amen" and its implication of self-surrender to welcome the life of Christ into his own life.

For Christian parents, this divine life has been given to their children through their own faith; now it needs to be awakened, strengthened, and developed as the child grows. Baptism has planted a seed of eternal life in the child; this seed has to grow through faith, hope and love for God and for all men. Just as a child becomes the citizen of the na-

All Christian parents must present their children for Baptism ...

tion through his parents, he also becomes a citizen of heaven, of a holy eternal nation, through his parents.

The baptism of an infant only finds justification if the parents have the faith of the Church which they can share with their children, for the infant has no conscience, no actual faith. Therefore, the Church accepts a child for Baptism on the guarantee that believing parents will share their own faith with their children. The Church's rule, therefore, is simple: all Christian parents must present their children for Baptism so that this sharing can take place. Thus, in the very ritual of baptism one of the great moments is the profession of faith which is a constitutive element of the sacrament.

The new rite of baptism expresses this emphasis on living faith very clearly at two specific moments. At the very beginning of the baptismal rite, the priest in the name of the Church, asks the parents: "What do you ask of God's Church?"

The parents reply: "Baptism."

The priest then delivers this warning: "You have asked to have your children baptized. In doing so you are accepting the responsibility of training them in the practice of the faith. It will be your duty to bring them up to keep God's commandments as Christ taught us, by loving God and our neighbor. Do you clearly understand what you are undertaking?"

At another moment, parents and sponsors are asked by the celebrant to proclaim their faith in the name of the child. This profession of faith in Christ is indispensable for the reception of Baptism.

The faith of the Church—which is asked by parents and sponsors for the infant and which is given by the Church to the infant—has meaning only if those who ask it for the child can share their own faith with the child. They must be prepared to fulfill their educational mission which they officially receive on this occasion.

It would be of the greatest value for everyone—Christian parents, catechists and priests—to take the necessary

time to analyze closely the new baptismal rite for infants.
Through such study Christian parents will rediscover the
grandeur of their mission in the Church, in the building up
of the Church.

Christian parents participate in fact in the triple mission which Christ has entrusted to the Church. They exercise their sacerdotal mission when they present their
children to the sacraments, not only Baptism but also Confirmation Eucharist and Penance. They exercise their
teaching and pastoral mission when they fulfill their duties
of Christian educators of their children.

Parents are indeed Christ for their children. Marriage is
a liturgy in itself, a function in the Church. Christian families
are not only a miniature of the Church but they constitute the Church as the living cells in which the
life of Christ exists. When Christian parents bring a child
to birth they can bring a child of God to birth, too. Christ
acts through them to transform the substance of humanity
into its divine fulfillment.

Practical conclusions flow from the theology of baptism
which is so beautifully expressed in the revised baptismal rite of infants. Today, the ceremony should focus on
parents as the ones to present their children to the Church
and to receive their children from the baptismal font, as
well as from the hands of the priest, representing Christ.
By fulfilling their liturgical functions, parents become conscious of who they are in the Church. It is through them
that their children have been presented to Christ, and it
is from the Church and before the community that parents are officially given their responsibility of being the
first catechists of the child.

In some cases, and after prudent and thorough pastoral action, pastors might have to decide that baptism of
children has to be refused. This would be the case where
absence of faith in the family gives little or no guarantee
for the post-baptismal education of the faith of the child.

The restoration of liturgical functions to Christian parents should not necessarily bring about the suppression of

god-parents. In spite of the questionable reasons for the introduction of sponsors that led to the exclusion of the parents at the baptism of their children, sponsorship is part of the development of the Church's tradition. There are no solid reasons to suppress it. Rather, it would seem better to increase the value of this function by requiring guarantees of faith and moral rectitude from those who will assist the parents in fulfilling their responsibilities.

Great pastoral care and liturgical education will be needed to emphasize the importance and presence of the Christian community at baptismal celebrations. The community is a visible sign of the faith of the Church that is transmitted to its new members. This has to be properly expressed.

The role of pastors and parish coordinators is to help Christian parents prepare for the baptism of their children, so that they might rediscover the grandeur of their educational mission. The Church must, in turn, assure them of the assistance which they have the right to demand of her, in order to fulfill this educational and catechetical responsibility.

It now becomes clear that Christian parents have the mission restored to them of preparing and presenting their children to the sacraments of the Christian initiation, such as Confirmation, the Eucharist, and, when the child has reached the necessary maturity, the Sacrament of Penance. For each sacrament, a parent-educator program should be made available through the parish. In connection with this last point, a re-evaluation of our educational religious institutions is also most desirable. Religious education has to extend beyond the institutions in which it has too exclusively taken refuge, namely the Catholic schools and CCD classes. It is necessary that a real collaboration be established between the home and the school of religion. Until recently, a catechetical formation of Christian parents has been non-existent. The role of the Church is not to relieve Christian parents of their legitimate rights and duties, but on the contrary, to help them in the full acceptance and accomplishment of their responsibilities. It is primarily through them that their children will encounter Christ in His Sacraments.

Chapter 3

The First Lesson: Love

*F*OR the child, Christian education begins in the cradle. For the parent, the basic and lasting lesson to teach is love. This means fulfilling the responsibilities of parenthood by answering the child's vital needs of safety and security in physical, psychological and emotional terms.

During the first six months, when the child depends totally on his parents for food and care, he experiences patterns of security and safety by the very fact that parents are there to answer his needs. When a mother has not answered those vital needs, a child builds up insecurity: he doesn't know what kind of a world he is in and he is afraid of the new world, rather than open to it.

By the seventh or eighth month when infants start recognizing physiognomies, parents should be extremely careful about who takes care of the children. It is disorienting to have different babysitters take care of our children: one day a young girl, next a grandmother, on another day a spinster. Each relates to the child and answers his needs of security and love and safety in very different ways. This leaves the child completely puzzled.

Routine is important and disruption painful to the infant. It's something that I make a point of watching for in my nieces and nephews. If my own brothers and sisters want to take off for a trip, or even if I visit with one of their

*I am on my way...I can trust the world in which I walk.
There is nothing I shall fear...*

infants, I always make a point of saying to the mother, "Tell me what's in your home and the routine you follow with your own child, so that I can pattern my day according to this routine. Otherwise I know I am doing real psychological harm to this child."

We start by eating a particular food, washing up and then resting. After that, we spend time in the playroom, go for a walk, and return, putting the clothes in a certain place. Lunch, a nap, a second walk, a snack, etc. Finally the whole routine of going to bed: is the special teddy bear or special doll on hand?

Because the child lives in the here and now and his immediate, recognizable world is so vitally important to him, a variation that passes unnoticed to an adult can be anxiety-producing for the infant. This does not mean that only *one* person is to be with the child. But it is extremely important that during the first year the child regularly experience the presence of a loving person, starting with his mother and people who can substitute for her by offering real love and concern. They must also be consistent with the mother's attitude and behavior.

A child has a crying need for uninterrupted love if he is ever going to grow into a person who can love in return. The whole Christian life and the whole process of growing up as a Christian revolves around the capacity to love, to love people in return and to love the Lord in return. In working with children who have been completely deprived of family environments and have been institutionalized, I have encountered the outcome—extremely aggressive behavior.

It is extremely important to take time with such children so they can experience love before they can ever respond with love. Children who have been scarred by life in an unhappy family also have a very hard time developing into genuine Christian persons. They have been exposed by the behavior of adults within their environment to lack of love, to tension, to evasions. This is the opposite of what we find in Corinthians 13, the great hymn of love where

St. Paul says: Love is forgiveness. Love is patience. Love is concern for the other. Love is the very small reality through which we find a way to express our love to the other.

From the beginning, the child needs a feeling of belonging and he needs to sense acceptance. When he feels fully accepted, when he feels family pride in his presence, a child will be able to develop into a person who can love in return.

Parents must feel and respond to the child's need of whether a child is an accident. Through non-verbal attitudes or passing comments we can devastate a child. A remark like, "Well, you were Number Seven; you arrived by accident," can be extremely traumatic for a child.

Parents must feel and respond to the child's need of belonging. Strangely enough, I have seen the best-intended parents overlook this need. They have three, four, five or six children, and fail to pay adequate attention to one or two of them. Maybe one child is not as good looking as another or has less pleasing mannerisms.

We all have our equal share in love and care . . .

Sometimes with my own brothers and sisters I have to call their attention to neglected members of the family unit. I say: "Now, your cute last little baby is the one that attracts all the attention. She is pretty and she is funny. Because she is the last to come into the family, she is the center of attraction, not only for her father and mother but also for her brothers and sisters. You have forgotten little Mary who is next to her in age, who hasn't a nice-looking face, who doesn't attract attention. Whenever little Mary is at the table and starts talking about what happened to her, someone stops her cold with the remark, 'We know.'" I always add: "Make sure you spread your love and that every child in the family receives the same care and concern, and that every child feels as much as any other that he belongs in the family."

Often as a teacher I have had children reflect a sense of rejection. This can show up in a drawing where the child draws a picture of his family and puts himself on the side, almost out of the picture. When asked why, the child will say, "Well, because I am the black sheep." When children have such feelings of rejection, their growth into sound Christian personalities is obstructed.

Next, the parent must respond to the child's need for self-esteem and self-respect. A child loves to grow, and during the pre-verbal stage he flowers under the recognition and encouragement of his family. A child's first step—surrounded by the cheering family, by the exultation of mother, father, brother, sister—announces a major breakthrough, the first step toward being on his own. It is a major move toward independence and its significance must not be lost on parents.

Parents must govern themselves accordingly. They must realize that the whole task of education, religious education in particular, is to help the child grow into greater and greater independence and freedom, into a greater and greater capacity to make free choices that are right choices. This places great demands upon adults because they have to watch the child take risks as he learns for himself how to walk downstairs, avoid hot radiators, hold a glass without dropping it. The parent must use prudence, of course, but he must avoid being over-protective or over-demanding.

Creativity is another need. One day the child will have to make responsible answers on the moral level, to make free personal decisions in full conscience. In order to have a child do this at a much later age, he must have the chance to be creative, to work independently at a much younger age. He starts out manipulating things with his hands. Holding a crayon is difficult at first for a child, but he should find out on his own. Don't impose a way on him; let him work according to his capacity.

A child's first drawings—sometime after the age of two—will be absolute nonsense for the adult, but what is important is that they have meaning for a child.

For instance, a child will bring a drawing to his parent

"That's how I see me and my house and the world. Please let me be me and tell you about it with crayons!"

and point it out as the family home—with no resemblance to the real thing. A misguided response would say: "This is not it; you did it wrong and I am going to show you how to draw a house." A child doesn't experience a house at all the way adults do, so you would then impose your vision of the world on him, thereby stifling him. Instead, the parent should respond to the drawings as a *valid* drawing of the house in a child's perspective.

Over-all, the first two years of Christian life can be summarized as a period of incalculable importance for future religious and human growth. That is why a child needs an atmosphere of security, love, belonging, creativity, peace and unity permeating everyday experiences, attitudes, gestures, words and actions in the home. This should be the basic emphasis of parents concerned with religious education at a very early age. They should be less concerned about knowing what they have to *tell* their children about Jesus and see to it that their children experience the love which the Spirit of Jesus has put into their own hearts.

The basic rule in religious education is to go from the simple to the more complicated, to go from what is implicitly experienced to what will be explicitly explained later on.

A child needs to be completely filled with the experience of love before he can make explicit within his own experience any reference to God the Father, Creator of Heaven and Earth. He needs this experience before he can discover the Son who comes and tells us in specific words how to love one another and the Spirit who lives in our hearts. The love encountered in the family can then be extended to the community, to the nation, to the family of men.

Chapter 4

Christianity without Words

IN the first two years of life, a child is surrounded by gestures, by signs of love, of joy, of laughter, even of reproof. It is the initial vocabulary which he masters, first by vaguely receiving it, dimly, then clearly getting the message. And finally, the child moves from the passive to the active tense. He returns gesture for gesture, sign for sign.

No mother forgets the first time that her baby smiles back. Parents, grandparents, brothers, sisters, relatives, and visitors are continuously smiling at babies; then one day a mother smiles and her baby smiles back. The love which surrounds the baby eventually elicits the positive response that says: "Yes, I want to communicate with you. I want to share love with you."

Through all the small gestures of parent-infant relationships, love is communicated in non-verbal language. These are the signs of love that also are the first signs of Christianity for the infant child. Adults clap their hands and extend their arms to a child, and an infant claps his hands and reaches out to be picked up. Think of the baby lying in his cradle, extending his arms, a gesture that says: "Pick me up and bring me close to you, into close, warm, comfortable contact with your body, for I realize that I belong to you and you belong to me. I belong to my father and he belongs to me. I belong to my brothers and sisters." You can just see

38

the joy expressed by the smile of a child who is passed from one set of loving arms to another, and through this very gesture he understands that he belongs. Through these very natural gestures, parents give their child the experience of belonging, for which he has such need and for which he is so hungry.

It all boils down to the need of people to be with people. Man has such a natural thirst to be loved and to be in contact with people. This starts from very early infancy, a need to which parents respond. How can we ever ask a child to love people, to love God and neighbor unless he has experienced this from the very beginning of his life?

Since the infant observes all the gestural language which people around him use to communicate, I would say that he receives his very first initiation into the life of prayer when he watches his family pray. He sees his father and mother, possibly brothers and sisters, in a mo-

We belong to one another . . .

ment of silence before praying together. They then speak to
a person whom they don't see, but who is there because he
sees there is communication going on through gesture and
language. This reverent silence followed by group praying
is extremely impressive to the young child.

It is particularly dramatic at mealtime. The very young
toddler who is permitted to sit in his high chair at the table
sees his family hold hands in a moment of silence and then
burst into a song, a song of joy, or praise for being united
around the table, for sharing this food. In so doing, they
show their love for one another, love which the child will
progressively be led to discover and love which is rooted
in the love of the Spirit, animating the family.

Little children join in prayer by the very fact that they
extend their hands and arms to be part of the group; they
don't want to be out of it, they want to be part of it. Here
is the very beginning of the experience of prayer.

There is another moment in the day when a parent can
use gestural language to impress on the child the experience of the adult relationship to God. It is when parents
bring a little baby to his room and put him to bed. There is
the very beautiful habit and gesture of a blessing on the
forehead. This sign is extremely meaningful for parents,
for they see that it is through them that the love and blessing of God are given to their children. Without them, their
child would be unable to develop into a loving and Christian person.

That sign of the cross on his forehead is deeply em-
bedded in the memory of a child. I often have heard adults
saying, "If I can remember one thing from my early childhood, it is the very ritualistic gestures I received from my
parents."

Bedtime, in particular, is a moment for a father or a
mother to show the child that he really belongs to them,
that they love him. The father and mother at that moment
might say in front of the child: "Heavenly Father, thank
you for giving me this child; keep us in your love and under
your loving care." Or anything else genuine that a parent

wants to express before his child.

There is no stereotyped formula. Every parent needs to think about the extraordinary dignity and mission he has received from God and express it in his own words before his child, holding his child in his own arms.

The morning is another crucial time of parent-infant prayer. In saying good morning, a mother can go to the window of the child's room and say in a very simple way, "Lord, all this day full of joy and beauty, I give to you. Thank you Lord, for this day we are going to spend together." The child doesn't understand a word but he does understand the solemn mood of his mother. Progressively, after having experienced this, the child will discover the meaning.

As the child progresses in the life of prayer, his first stage of participation is imitation. The toddler extending his

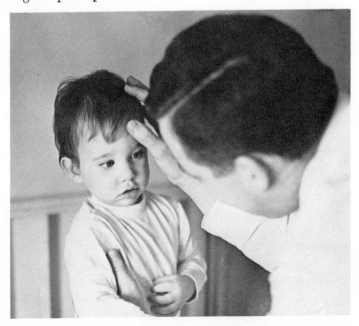

"Good night ... May God our Father keep us in His loving care."

hand during grace before meals is making his own initial gesture of prayer. After imitating movements, the child will hum along until the day he is able to pop in with a word or two, and then join in for whole sentences.

Another bodily, non-verbal language important to the child occurs on the first visit to church. It can be casual, a stopover while shopping, an extension of the walk in the park. What is important on such an occasion? Just to observe a moment of silence. Listen how silence is filled with reality. It is vital that the child appreciate silence and learn to listen to silence.

A mother can also kneel down with reverence, possibly near the altar, pray for a minute—pray before the child genuinely, not posturing, but really praying. The child will do nothing but look at his parent, realizing that this is really an important moment, that he is in a very special place.

Here we have the foundation of private prayer and the desire of man to bring some peace and some silence into his day in order to be able to listen to the Lord. Silence is the first prerequisite for prayer so that the Lord can speak to us before we ever utter a word in response.

Christian feast days are special occasions for the learning of prayer. At Christmastime, the infant watches the family go up to the crib in the home, genuflect and remain in a silent, stationary position. When gifts are exchanged, when there is carol singing, the child shares in the celebration by sensing the special joy in the home. On Good Friday, the child will watch the Cross prepared for veneration in the home; on Easter morning, the child will hear a joyful Alleluia. I make a point in my family's home of playing a record of Handel's Hallelujah Chorus from *The Messiah* so that the tiny child is impressed by the very sounds of exultation.

Thus, at a very early age a parent can educate his child to prayerful attitudes through gestures. Not only is a small child ready to pray with this sign language, which is the sole language available to him, but the experiences are tiny stepping stones to a level of participation in a worshipping community.

With both prayer and bodily gestures, a Christian community expresses praise, thanksgiving, offering to God. It is noteworthy that the Church is rediscovering this gestural language today in and through the liturgy. The laity, in turn, is demanding that pastors and priests use a more meaningful, beautiful, and precise liturgical gesture so that the full message is communicated. Such are the signs of Christianity to be found in the nursery as well as the cathedral.

Father,... show me how to pray...

Chapter 5

Christianity in
Picture and Statue

AN infant in his crib looks on a small universe of familiar
faces and surroundings, whose particular boundaries are
four walls and a ceiling. Where do religious pictures and
statues belong in the cramped universe of the infant's
room? What representations of the Christian mystery should
an infant look up and see from his crib? Which Christian art
and pictures belong in a child's room?

Actually, the preceding chapters have shown that the
child's first living image of God is that of a loving father
and mother. These are the two most impressive images that
will influence the child's future belief and Christian commitment.

But Christian parents should not underestimate the impact of visual aids to develop the Christian message. For
centuries, the Church has used this powerful tool to instruct
the faithful. We only have to look at the Gothic cathedrals;
in an age when few people could read, the Church used the
language of pictures to teach them the history of Salvation.
Here we see the story of God depicted in sculpture, in
stained glass windows, in paintings and frescoes.

Questions about the use of religious art and pictures in
the home are asked time and again by Christian parents,
particularly those conscientious parents who look back with

44

a critical eye at some pictures and statues which filled their own rooms and homes when they were young children.

Parents can no longer remain passive about this issue. Especially today, with the "new plastic age," there has come a degrading of religious representation that is frightening. Too often in our quest for bargains we have accepted new horrors at special low prices. If we wish to avoid reducing the Christian mystery to the level of playthings, gimmicks and good-luck charms, we have to react and become more demanding in regard to artistic quality and theological truth. Also many of us have an understandable affection for objects of our childhood, but that does not mean they were all good.

Parents, ... you are the first pictures of God's love for your children ... for God is love and you are made in His image and likeness ...

We know that learning starts at the level of concrete sensorial experiences. Each of us first experiences life through the senses before we can form a concept and understand it. Religious drawings by children themselves show the impact of visual aids in conveying the faith.

If Christian art is educational, then, its educational content is co-existent with its theological and artistic content. All religious art that serves the religious education of the faithful has, therefore, to be evaluated according to its theological correctness, its aesthetic quality and its psychological compatibility. This last point is especially true when dealing with very young children whose first impressions and experiences are of the greatest importance for the future.

Different pitfalls are to be avoided. We can, for instance, find pictures that are real masterpieces of art but in which theological content is distorted (*i.e.*, some pictures of the Last Judgment). Others, instead, might be theologically correct but artistically immature (i.e., some syrupy paintings of Christ). We find pictures that are both theologically correct and good art yet are psychologically unfitting for a child's sensitivity (*i.e.*, some over-dramatic representations of the Crucifixion or saints undergoing martyrdom). Finally, we have representations that are both poor art and poor theology (*i.e.*, some plastic statues used as magical charms to ward off traffic accidents).

If parents are attentive to these different norms in religious pictures, they will ultimately come to choose quality over quantity. Let's be more specific. We should first of all search for pictures that represent the core of the Christian mystery. Let's examine the central events of Christian faith and evaluate their representation in art and use in a child's room.

The core of the Good News proclaimed by Christ's disciples to the nations is the resurrection of Jesus Christ. It is around this mystery that the Gospel has developed and where the faith of the Christians is rooted.

In terms of the centrality and the actuality of the

resurrection, what do we find on the walls of our children's rooms? I am afraid the answer is "nothing." Most often the Risen Lord has been screened off by the colorful wings of a guardian angel or else we will find him represented as a baby Jesus. With the very best intentions, parents and god-parents think that because a child is a child, Christ has to be brought down to the level of the child, and therefore presented as a little child. Not only that, rather than as a Jewish child, he is represented as a blond, blue-eyed Germanic child. You would never recognize Jesus' origin in Palestine, born of a Jewish mother.

The need to represent a "baby" Jesus to young children reveals a psychological misunderstanding of what a child is and through which processes it grows into a mature person. Any parent or kindergarten teacher observing the play of a child will notice that as soon as he is able to utter a few words and master gestural language, he will play the role of an adult. Children playing together will say: "I am the mother," and "You are the father." The whole dynamism of the child is oriented toward becoming an adult and it is through identification with big people that little people grow up.

If a mother wants to impress her young child with the actual existence and love of a father, who has left for a long journey, which picture of her husband will she choose? That of the cute little baby he once was, years ago? Or that of the adult man he is today? Therefore, which picture of Christ should we present? The Baby Jesus or the Risen Lord? It is obvious that the goal of each Christian is his identification with the Risen Lord. So, too, should be the goal set for the Christian child.

It is for this reason that we should avoid presenting as a first picture of Christ that of a small pink, curly baby Jesus. What the child needs is the picture of a person the child can respect and with whom he will want to identify. A picture of the Risen Lord that is at the same time an art reproduction is what is needed for the family living room and the children's bedrooms. Such pictures exist, although we

may have to look in art books or art gift shops. Some repro-
ductions of Christ in Glory can be found in the statues of
great cathedrals. The Eastern church has a magnificent art
tradition representing the Lord Jesus. Christ is portrayed as
an adult with an extraordinary piercing quality in his gaze.
He is a true man who very often holds a book in his hand
to show that he is a teacher; yet beyond the human characteristics, one can perceive the mystery and majesty of divinity that is expressed through the use of gold, the un-
worldly colors and the facial expression. Some contemporary Christian artists, who have rediscovered the centrality
of the resurrection in their own lives, have through some
beautiful art represented the same mystery of Christ.

What is important is that through non-verbal visual language the truth of the mystery of Christ is experienced.
There will come, at a later time, the day when parents and
teachers will teach explicitly what has been implicitly
experienced.

Should we then in early childhood totally exclude pictures representing the baby Jesus? Obviously, if we want to
be faithful to the message given through the Gospel, the answer is "no." In this matter, however, let's follow the prior-
ity the Gospel writers have given us. The core of the
preaching of the Church is centered around the resurrection. The first parts written in the Gospels are those of the
resurrection narratives. It was only later, when the narratives of the public life of Christ had been recorded, that
two of the evangelists recorded the narratives of the infancy
of Jesus. Why not follow their example? In this matter, let
us also follow the example of the Church which celebrates
the mystery of Christ all through the liturgical year.

Christmas is certainly the best time in the year to introduce young children to the infant Jesus and the mystery
of his Incarnation. In Chapter Nine of this book, parents will
find examples of how to present the Child Jesus to young
children. What is important is that through our exposition
the child grasps that Jesus is truly a person like anyone of
us. He became a baby like us; he grew like us; he needed a

"Before the world was created the Word already existed...
the Word became a human being and lived among us...
we saw His glory full of grace and truth..."— Jn. 1.

mother and father to take care of him, like us; he needed
sleep; he needed to learn how to work, to read, to write.
Then one day, when he was a grown-up man the time came
when his Father wanted him to leave home and start his
mission of preaching and inaugurating the Kingdom of
Heaven.

When Christmas is past and we have celebrated the
coming of the Kings on the Day of the Epiphany, we remove the crib and change the visual aids in our living room
to coincide with the liturgical year. Then we can have the
next steps—a picture of the teaching Christ coming at the
Lenten season, the Cross of Victory to replace the teaching
Christ when we come to Holy Week, and finally at Easter
a reproduction of the Risen Lord associated with the word,
"Alleluia!"

The presentation of Christ's mystery would not be
complete if we exclude the event of Christ's death, as a step
towards his resurrection. The representation of the crucifixion, which most often includes a corpse on a cross, needs
to be re-evaluated by Christian parents from a psychological as well as from a theological point of view.

Personally, I have often noted children's reactions to
the crucifixion by watching their facial expressions and
hearing their first words before the corpse of Christ on the
cross. The first time I realized the effects a picture of the
crucifixion can have on a young child was fifteen years ago,
on a Sunday afternoon.

The incident involved a nephew who had been nap-
ping in my parents' home. The child, who was just beginning to talk, took his nap in a very narrow, little room
where my mother kept her discarded things, including all
kinds of holy pictures. Theologically and esthetically, they
were not the best, but because they had been given to her
by some friend, nun or priest and had been blessed, she
didn't feel she could throw them away. In addition, a crucifix was hanging over the little bed, where for six months the
child had been taking an afternoon nap. As I came into the
room and opened the curtains to let in some light, I saw

him gazing at the crucifix. Out popped what had gone through his eyes and mind for no one knows how long, "Jesus . . . man . . . dead . . . sad."

His words gave me a shock. It is wrong for a child's first experience of Christ to be that of a dead man on a cross, instead of as a Risen Lord. The center of faith is not a dead man but One Who is fully alive. The child needs to learn first that the Lord is risen and is alive. Instead, as my nephew's experience of six months of staring reminded me, we confront our children with a lifeless corpse hanging from a cross.

There is certainly a need to re-evaluate this Western tradition of hanging crucifixes in the rooms of little children. I fear it is not a sound introduction to the total mys-

An embarrassing question . . . "Jesus . . . ? A dead man? . . . How sad . . . !"

tery of Christ's death and resurrection. Moreover, some realistic representations of the crucifixion (with emphasis on blood, thorns, nails, etc.) can be traumatic, especially to a little child, unable to grasp its full meaning in context.

One Holy Week, my brothers and sisters decided to do something about this and what they did suggests a better approach towards the Crucifixion in terms of children. They decided to remove the crucifixes with corpses from the children's rooms. They set about making crosses as replacements. On Good Friday, the parents took the children into the garden to collect pieces of wood so that each child could make his own cross for his room, while the parents themselves would make a large cross for the living room.

This provided activity and creativity for the children as they searched for different shapes and different textures, different kinds of wood to make their crosses. The crosses were simple. Those who could manage with nails used nails, others used strings. After each cross was assembled, each child devised his own way of showing that it was through the cross that Jesus achieved victory over death and gave joy and everlasting life to the world. Some nephews and nieces made banners with very colorful and glorious colors to put up as a background for their crosses; others strung together dried flowers to form a crown to decorate the Cross —crowns of victory. Others used palms from Palm Sunday to make a wreath of victory. In this way, the cross became what it should be—a sign of victory over death and sin, a sign of achieving glory.

Christians through the centuries have always represented the Mother of God in picture and we would fail Christian tradition if we omitted to present Mary to our children in our homes. What is important from a theological point of view is to associate closely the mystery of Mary with the Mystery of Christ and of the Church. An isolated devotion to Mary might distort our whole understanding of the Christian mystery.

Mary is primarily the mother of God.

Therefore, it is extremely important to select a picture of Mary with her Son. The truth we are teaching is that Mary is the one who brings Christ into the world.

Unfortunately, the nineteenth century separated the devotion to Mary from her son, Jesus. Many pictures which we find in our homes are inspired by that tendency to represent Mary alone. This is a distortion from what is central to a sound Marian spirituality: Mary leads us to her Son, she leads us to Christ, she is a servant who always says, "Look to Him! Listen to His Word. Do what He says."

Once again, the norm for choosing a religious picture combines the theologically correct and aesthetically beautiful. Never present a picture of Our Lady which is poor art! If we do, we damage something extremely important in our children—the aesthetic feeling which, if well-fed by good religious art or religious music, is close to religious experience. We should provide this aesthetic nourishment at an early stage of development, as well as in the later stages. Never give the child something he will have to reject for aesthetic or theological reasons later in life.

There is also the worthy tradition of giving children

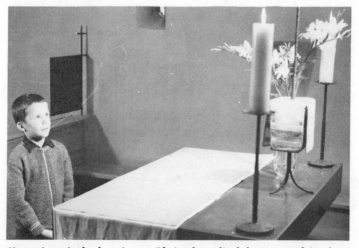

Keep in mind, that Jesus Christ has died for us and is risen from the dead ... He is our Savior, He is life, love and joy for all men.

pictures of the patron saints after whom they are named. Unfortunately, there are not too many beautiful pictures of saints.

The Guardian Angel presents a particular problem. Often, in our teaching and through pictures the Guardian Angel emerges as the central point of a child's religious visual experience. True, a picture of the Guardian Angel has great appeal in its promise of security. But this is done at the expense of presenting the parent as the source of immediate security, of presenting the Holy Spirit who is within us and to whom we can speak at any moment, of presenting Christ as the shepherd who leads us on the right paths of life.

Moreover, most pictures of Guardian Angels present an image so colorful and so powerful that it overwhelms the central truths of Christianity. Because the Guardian Angel is peripheral to Christian faith and life, pictures of him should recede into the background, so that Christ can reach the foreground.

Sometimes, the Guardian Angel is depicted in holy pictures along with the devil. The Guardian Angel is on the right suggesting good things to do; the devil is on the left suggesting all kinds of naughty things to do. The child sees himself in between the two voices and faced with a choice between the good and bad angels.

It is advisable to do away with all representations of the devil. Before a young child is ever faced with sin and its associate, the devil, he should first be introduced to goodness in life, to how he can be happy and make others happy, to how he can please the Lord. Pictures of the devil provoke fantasies about hell and eternal damnation which can be disturbing for a young child, who has not committed sin and who can not even sin for many years.

At baptism, godparents often give the child a medal. It is a sign of putting on Christ or a sign expressing the fact that the child has received the spirit of Christ through baptism. I have seen very beautiful medals symbolizing the Trinity or the Holy Spirit. Medals are certainly an appropriate custom, provided that nothing is said to indicate that the medal has magical power, which I'm afraid, all too many people assign to them.

In short, what we are saying is that parents who are concerned about preparing their children for adult Christian behavior should not try to foster faith linked to accidentals, but should give their children the essence of our religion: Christ. He is the solid rock on which to build the faith of every child.

"Hosannah in the highest. Blessed is He, who comes in the name of the Lord, hosannah in the highest!"

What about pictures of God the Father?

In general, I would observe the rule of Israel which is very specific on religious art: you shall never make a picture of the God of Israel, of the Father and the God of Abraham, Isaac and Jacob. Pictures of God the Father almost universally are theologically wrong. One familiar picture for little children depicts our heavenly Father as an old, white-haired, bearded man who floats over the world with a very serious look. He is like a supreme policeman looking for the chance to catch us whenever we do something naughty so that he can punish us. This impression completely contradicts the first experiences a child has of his own father, and should have, through him, of his heavenly Father. The first true image and experience a child should have of his heavenly Father is that he is a true and living image of a loving father and mother who care for their children and are willing to forgive, ready to bring their children back to the right way and help them through life. Therefore, we should avoid pictorial representations of God the Father as He who punishes.

Another familiar and distorted representation of God the Father and the Trinity is the triangle in which you see an eye with rays of glory shining from it. Such an extremely abstract symbol doesn't mean anything to a child, and certainly a geometrical figure is no way to express the loving relationships between three persons who love one another to the extent that their love embraces all mankind!

The Holy Spirit suffers similarly from misrepresentation in holy pictures. The Holy Spirit is a spiritual reality, hidden but active, in the heart of man and is approached only through silence and through attentiveness to his dynamic presence within us. He is more intimate to myself than myself, present in the very heart of man. To depict the invisible and spiritual reality of the Holy Spirit is impossible.

In a child's room both religious objects and toys belong, but there could be a place set aside as a prayer corner —a place to say evening prayers and to keep religious objects. Some respect should be connected with religious objects by the very fact that we hang them in a prominent place in a child's room. The child's prayer corner is also a place for his creative art as a response to the need of prayer. Such art represents his discovery of a sign of God's omnipotence and goodness in and through his creation, particularly his people. For instance, if a child has painted flowers, the picture can be placed in the prayer corner as a reminder

"I am the Lord's servant," said Mary (Luke 1:38). That is why she is chosen to become the mother of God.

that we are going to thank God for these beautiful flowers.

Photographs of people we want to pray for also have a place in the child's room. As children become aware of social problems and social difficulties in the world at large, it would be relevant to pray for an outcome or an event. A picture depicting an event or situation could be placed on the wall either in the family room or in the child's room. In this way, secular events are related to the child's life of prayer and will help him grow into a mature believer for whom every aspect and event of life has a Christian dimension.

Finally, there is the Bible, *the* book which should not only be on a shelf in our library but should be given a place of honor in our living room. The reading of the Bible should be approached with reverence. The physical presence of the Bible and the reverence with which it is approached will have an important influence on a small child. A lighted candle alongside the Bible symbolizes the light we need in order to find meaning in our own life and in the life of all mankind. The candle, the Bible, the atmosphere of reverence, the visual signs of Christianity—all these bring the tiny child to the threshhold of Christianity with words.

Chapter 6

Christianity in Prayer and Song

*B*ECAUSE children invariably bring adults to the point of confronting their own faith and practice, the question of prayer sorely challenges parents. In raising the matter of children's prayer, we bring up the matter of adult prayer. Do we pray? Does a wife pray with her husband? Do parents pray before their children? Or do parents have to acknowledge that prayer doesn't play a vital role in their home and family life?

The problem is real, for prayer is, in fact, not a natural and easy activity. The person who prays needs to begin with a moment of silence in order to open himself to the Word of God, to God who wants to speak to him. The person who prays doesn't speak. Moreover, through the eyes of a child a person who prays seems to be in the presence of an invisible person. Prayer is an original encounter with a living person who is more intimate to myself than myself. Prayer is a true encounter with my God in the deepest part of my person.

The little child who has seen his parents in this moment of silence before speaking to that invisible person is initiated already into the secret of prayer. He is initiated into this secret in his family experience. He will build on the experience of seeing his parents, brothers and sisters pray together.

As a baptized child, as a son of God, he will some day be called to share this intimate encounter with the Lord. The very young child needs the adults and his older brothers and sisters around him to perceive the presence of God in his life. He shares in their prayerful attitudes, then, progressively, in the words.

In a Christian family, the little one starts participating in the prayer of the family by gesture. He will next mumble some sound to join in. Parents should not be concerned about prayer formulas. It is much more important that the little child share in the family atmosphere, that he perceive through his senses, through his eyes, through his ears, that something very important is going on.

Parents must respect the child's development and at each stage help him to express his new experiences and relationship in and through prayer. Three significant stages can be emphasized. The first stage starts in the child's life itself. The second stage involves awakening of the child to the sense of the sacred. The third stage is initiation of the child in the prayer of the Christian community, more specifically, the worshiping community. Clearly these three different stages in the child's life of prayer are not clear-cut; they overlap one another as the child develops broader consciousness.

The first stage involves the child's life experiences, the source of his knowledge. Before he ever goes to school, the main interests and experience of the young child are limited to his environment. From his room and from his relationship with his parents during early infancy, he will extend his experience to the house, to brothers and sisters, to people, children and all the people in the neighborhood. His prayer life will enlarge more and more as his social and concrete experiences expand from the home.

A mother can start to pray with her two-year-old child by discovering a beautiful sunrise from the window of his room and by extending her arms along with the arms of the child to express a prayer of praise to the Lord. As the child becomes three or four years old, prayer will extend to

Where two or three are together in love there I am . . .

other experiences and concerns: little friends in the neighborhood or in nursery school; shopping trips with one of his parents; meeting neighborhood people such as the mailman or milkman.

Long before he is six, the mass media have brought in the outside world. He will watch an earthquake over television or the suffering which wars bring into the world. His parents can help him to relate this actuality and these experiences to the Christian vision and the Christian message to the world. They can tell and they can show a small child how a Christian reacts to all this.

The opportunities for children's prayer are numerous in the course of a day. The child of two or three who stays with his mother at home very naturally expresses what he feels: he tells her when he is happy and when he is sad. He runs to his father or mother for protection, he enjoys sitting on their laps and feeling their warm love and concern for him.

Parents can sometimes take the opportunity and the experience of very close contacts to say, "Isn't it good to be in our home together? Father and mother are here to protect you. God is here to protect you also." Or else, "Aren't you happy now that Daddy is home? How good it is to be with Daddy! How good it is to be with God our Father!"

Before leaving the room after putting her child to bed, a mother can say: "We have had a wonderful day together; now I leave you and you can speak to Jesus for He is with you." Or a father can say to his child at bedtime: "Jesus is with you; He watches over you because He loves you."

In taking the opportunity to use daily events to help their children pray to the Lord, parents should avoid certain pitfalls. They should not take advantage of *every* occasion, of *every* experience, to pray with their children or to relate an experience to the Christian message. They should watch for the favorable moment in the child's life to make an explicit reference to God. This varies according to the temperament of the child, the circumstances, the age.

A child of three says everything that he feels, while a child of five is more reserved. Parents should respect the stage in which their children are. On the other hand, an adult sees significance in many events which pass completely beyond the awareness of children. It is therefore useless to try to create an artificial link between those daily events and the prayer life of children. A parent must discriminate among pictures and events shown on TV and know which ones are relevant to the child.

Another danger is to take advantage—however well-meaning—of children's sensitivity. A young child loves to love and lives in very close sympathy with whatever or whoever is in his environment; it is therefore a real temptation for parents to base prayer on the emotionality or the sensitivity of the child.

"God is love and whoever lives in love lives in God
and God lives in him" (John 4:16).

It is tempting to say, for instance, "Let us pray for the babies who have no mothers," or "Let us pray for the mothers whose children have been killed." This is dangerous procedure, for it abuses the sensitivity of children. It is sincere, but it plays an emotional trick upon the child and such devices eventually backfire. Parents should avoid approaches toward prayer that a child will later reject as an adolescent.

Nor should regular prayer be a blind, unbending routine. On certain nights, for instance, the family may be tired after a long trip or there may be company for dinner or the family may be up unusually late. Rather than force prayer upon children when they are excessively tired or when circumstances interfere with a suitable atmosphere, parents can simply put off prayer for that evening. Another can say: "We're so tired tonight that we will go to bed quickly. Everyone simply say good night to the Lord." Or a father might say: "We have guests tonight for dinner. We will not be able to pray together so will you please speak to the Lord when you are in your room?"

Sometimes, children categorically refuse to pray. Before imposing their will upon them, parents should reflect for a moment on such questions as these: Has this particular prayer been repeated so long that it is losing meaning? Does this prayer which satisfied a three-year-old suit a six-year-old? Is it more appropriate to have the child pray alone in silence? In this context, it is worth recalling the words of Jesus who needed to pray alone on the mountain:

> "But when you pray, go into your room and shut the door and pray to your Father who is in secret, and your Father who sees in secret will reward you.
> "And in praying, do not heap up empty phrases as the Gentiles do, for they think that they will be heard for their many words."   (Matthew VI:6-7)

I learned an unforgettable lesson in this regard from a 10-year-old nephew and it applies to children of all ages.

"I love the sound of silence . . ."

It happened early one Sunday morning when my nephew and his younger brother were staying overnight with their grandmother as was often their custom. When the weather was nice, I would hear them creep out of the house and then walk side by side along the pond in the garden. They walked in absolute silence.

One morning I joined them in their silent stroll. After watching the pond and looking at the sun rising, in a mood of meditation, my nephew turned to me and said, "Aunt Christiane, you're sometimes unhappy because I don't join in prayers at home aren't you? I can't pray when we are around the table, but you know when I really can pray? It is right now. I can pray when I watch the sun coming over the pond; I can pray when I hear the birds sing; what about you, Anthony?"

Anthony, his younger brother, didn't say a word but showed through his smile that this, too, was a way he could praise and pray and speak to the Lord. This silent environment was the most conducive to prayer for them. What better illustration of these words from Mark (1:35)—"And in the morning, a great while before day, He rose and went out to a lonely place and there He prayed."

Parents can also help children learn to pray by acknowledging their own difficulties in praying. They can say: "You know, sometimes I'm really very, very tired and need lots of effort to pray." In this way children understand that prayer is not easy and that it needs preparation, a proper use of silence, the right atmosphere, and that it can only take place at certain moments of the day.

The vocabulary of prayer should be taken from the familiar world of the child. Pious jargon may be a habit, but it is by no means sacred. For little children, the most familiar words are best. For instance, "Jesus, I'm happy. I love you." Or before sleeping: "Thank you, Jesus, for this beautiful day, for the sun, for the flowers that have come out, for my cat."

Or parents can tell their children, "Pray to the Lord and thank him for people—Thank you, Jesus, for Daddy and

Mother, for my little brother Anthony, for my older sister Jeanie." Events and visits by loved ones can be inserted into the evening prayer; for instance, "Thank you, Jesus, for Daddy and Mother, for my little brother Anthony, for my grandmother who came today, and for the candy she brought with her."

Sometimes at night parents have a chance to talk to children about their day; maybe there was a difficult and naughty moment involving a brother or playmate. Parents can help children develop their moral conscience by asking forgiveness of the Lord by praying in the following way: "Jesus, it was hard for me to share my toys with Anthony today. Please help me tomorrow to share them with him."

Progressively, children will join in with specifically religious words which are used in the liturgy and in family prayer. In observing my own nieces and nephews, as well

Parent and children discover the beauty of flowers...

as other children, I have noticed that the first liturgical words they learn are Amen and Alleluia. They hear Amen at the end of family prayers. My little nephew stops me when I am leaving for church and asks: "May I come along with you to say Amen to the Lord?"

Children love to learn new words, even foreign words. I like to tell them that I'm going to teach them new words from a different language than ours, words with which we can speak to the Lord. To the very basic Christian and liturgical words or songs, we should add a few carefully-selected verses adapted from Holy Scripture.

The child enjoys prayers which have a beautiful poetical form, particularly the Psalms. Psalms use a concrete and very suggestive language; they feed the imagination of the child. If sung, they bring joy to both adults and children. Children will never have to reject this kind of prayer, even if in their early childhood the words of the Psalms go beyond their understanding. As the child matures, he will reach a deeper and deeper appreciation for these words and will be able to carry on with this prayer through his adolescence into a mature adult Christian life in prayer. As a child is introduced into a worshiping community he will master this special vocabulary and it will help him feel at home.

The spontaneous and traditional prayers of the church which parents can share with pre-school children, fall into four categories: prayers of thanksgiving, trust, forgiveness and petition.

Prayers of thanksgiving are natural for a young child who is discovering people and things around him. Parent and child discover together the beauty of a flower, or the joy of a meadow in which a dog is romping, or the wonder of the moon and stars at night. This can be a unique opportunity to say: "How great, how beautiful the Lord is. Alleluia." And one could sing "We give Thee thanks, Oh God, our Father. Sing your praise to God."

(Music and words from the Hymnal)

Or on Easter Day when all the daffodils are in the meadows and in the public parks, parents can teach their children to sing these words and music from the Hymnal:

Besides nature, parents should teach children to praise the Lord for people and for the works of man. For example, parents can say with their children after seeing a beautiful bridge: "We praise You, Lord, for making man so intelligent that he can build a car. We praise You, Lord, for those men who help build the bridges. Glory to You, oh Lord, for the mind and for the body of men. Thank You, Lord, for their work."

Cities are also rich in contacts and experiences; movies, radio and television offer other ways to discover the greatness of God. It is important to put the accent on the positive values which we find in all urban, suburban, or rural modes of life and to express this clearly in prayer to the Lord. He has made the world for man to enjoy and one should constantly repeat this to children—"And God saw that all was good."

Another form of prayer in which parents should prepare children is the prayer of confidence, of trust in the Lord. A young child has great need for security; therefore,

prayers of trust are indispensable for him. Whatever difficulties he meets, a young child must know he is loved by
God. Simple prayers, like the following, address themselves
to the need:

"Lord, today has been a hard day, but I know You
love me; I know You're always with me. I put all my
trust in You, oh Lord."

Or parents can teach children by singing "The Lord is
always with me; He is my shepherd. Nothing shall I fear."

"My soul is longing for the Lord; near to You, oh
Lord, there is the place where I want to be."

"My heart is waiting for the Lord; in Him I put all my
hope and trust."

"Into Your hands, oh Lord, my God, I give You my
day, all that I am and do."

Or these quotations can be adapted from the Psalms:

My God, I want You with all my heart
Do not let me wander away from You.
Teach me to do what You want;
I want to listen to what You say.
I want to do the things that please You
So that I may be Your friend forever. (Psalm 118)

Deep down in my heart I ask You. Lord,
Give me Your strength.
I will do all that I can to please You,
Always and everywhere.   (Psalm 18)

I am not afraid of anything
When I am with the Lord
Because a child who is with the Lord
Stands in the light and
His face is radiant with joy.   (Psalm 33)

A child should never feel that God will rebuff him and
turn from him for wrong-doing, for being mean or for being
naughty. Instead, the child should feel that God is always
seeking him, calling him back to His love so that once again

they can be friends. That is the significance of prayers of
forgiveness. A few verses of Psalm 50 could be taken and
adapted for children in this manner:

> Lord, I have turned away from you but
> I am sorry for that, and I ask you to
> forgive me.
> Lord, call me back to you and I will
> return because you are always willing
> to forgive.

Or else,

> My God, open my heart and change it,
> And my heart shall be full of joy.

The very act of forgiveness by parents is a sign of
God's willingness to forgive children. Parents can express
the joy of forgiveness by taking, for instance, some excerpts
of Psalm 31, and saying them with the child:

> How happy I am because God has forgiven
> whatever I did wrong.
> Lord, I know that I did wrong and I
> said to myself, 'I will tell it to the
> Lord,' and now everything is forgiven;
> my heart is full of joy.

Another prayer of forgiveness could be:

> Rejoice, rejoice in the Lord and
> Sing his praises
> Now that your heart is new and happy
> Because you have been forgiven.

If a child has made peace with a brother, sister or friend
after a quarrel, he can remember this event at night with
Psalm 18:

> I offer You, oh Lord, this prayer:

Let me love You more and more,
Let me love others more and more.
Thank You for their love and their
Forgiveness.

Or else:

Lord, give me Your strength
So that I can do all the things
That please You.
So that I can do all the things
That please my parents, my friends.
(Here a child can mention the names of those he wants to please.)

Among songs expressing the desire of the child to be forgiven by both parents and the Lord are:

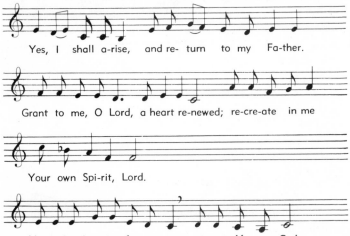

Yes, I shall a-rise, and re- turn to my Fa-ther.

Grant to me, O Lord, a heart re-newed; re-cre-ate in me

Your own Spi-rit, Lord.

My soul is long-ing for your peace, near to You, my God.

Parents may be surprised to find the prayer of petition listed as the last form of prayer for young children. That is because children should be introduced first to prayers of praise, of trust and of forgiveness before they are introduced to the prayer of petition, which is the most difficult prayer to present in a proper context.

Because a child is centered upon himself and is in an egocentric stage, he naturally tries to put the Lord at his service. This tendency is aggravated by parents who tell their child to pray in the following manner: "Lord, please heal grandfather" or "Lord, give us nice weather tomorrow," or "Lord, give me beautiful toys at Christmas." Such egocentric petitions strengthen the child's concept of God as a magic maker working for him.

Asking the Lord for something is not the same as asking a father for a bicycle. The basic attitude is totally different. Petitions to the Lord are always oriented toward God's will; they ask that His Will be done. If we pray to

Photos offer ways to discover the greatness of God . . .

the Lord for someone who is dying, for someone who is
sick, for a little sister who is in the hospital, it is mainly to
share with Him our concern for that person. It is mainly to
tell Him how much we love that person and how deeply
we are affected by the suffering of that person.

Prayers of petition should be reasonable, truly human,
and should show respect for the divine. It is quite normal
for children to pray to the Lord when a grandfather has
died or when a little sister has gone to the hospital. But the
focus should be on those who need God's strength to accept this suffering. If a little sister, for instance, has had an
accident and has had to enter the hospital, let us pray that
she may be patient and recover quickly. Let us pray for our
grandmother so that she can offer to the Lord the sacrifice
of her lost husband. Let us also pray with our children for
those who are alone. Then let us act upon that prayer by
visiting those who are alone.

We also pray for peace in the world, but peace begins
at home in the neighborhood. Parents should lead their
children to ask the Lord to give them the necessary strength
to make peace with their brothers and with their little
friends in the neighborhood. In this way, the prayer of petition merges with the prayer of trust. If someone is very
sick and dying, don't ask the Lord for a miracle. Ask Him,
rather, to give that person and those who love him strength
in their distress.

It is extremely important for parents to add gestures
to prayers. More and more these gestures will be oriented
toward the gestures used in the liturgy. Through bodily attitudes and gestures, a child will most deeply and intuitively
discover the sacred sense.

As a catechist of children, I have never found the
right words to explain to them the glory, the greatness, and
the magnitude of God, or what it means for man to adore
the Lord. But I have found I was able to give them the
right understanding of the greatness and sacredness of the
Lord by kneeling down in adoration. They would look at
me, listen to the few words which I said to the Lord, and

sense the deep attitude of adoration which I tried to express in front of them. They then would ask me to help them assume the proper bodily attitude to express their adoration from the depths of their own being.

Prayer involves a deep reality that is indescribable. You just cannot communicate it with words alone. Gestural language helps to express deep feelings of adoration, praise, and thanksgiving. Bodily attitudes, silence, symbols, and religious environment—all help a child enter the life of prayer.

Walking with a young child in church, a parent can bow solemnly before the altar and say or sing: "Lord, how little we are before You, for You alone are holy. You alone are great. You alone are the most High." During evening or morning prayers, a parent can say: "Lord, we are extending our hands," or sing in the morning: "Lord, all that I shall

*In introducing little children to the life of prayer,
parents must be sincere...*

do, all that I am, I give You, today, for everthing belongs
to You, oh Lord."

Lifting up our arms is a powerful means of expressing
an attitude of praise, adding gestures to words and songs.
Some examples:

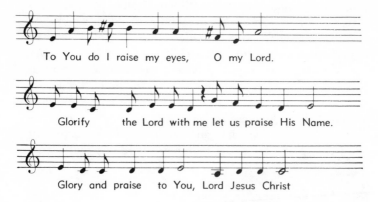

To You do I raise my eyes,   O my Lord.

Glorify   the Lord with me let us praise His Name.

Glory and praise   to You, Lord Jesus Christ

Give praise to the Lord, all you men, Alleluia.
Oh praise the name of the Lord, Alleluia.
Blessed be the name of the Lord, Alleluia.
Alleluia.

In introducing little children to the life of prayer, parents must be sincere, they must be genuine. Children
should never be asked to *perform* their prayers for the sake
of their parents or any other adults. We do not ask children
to pray *before* us. It is we who pray before them and *along
with them.* Our words will become the children's words,
our gestures will become the children's gestures, our attitudes will become the children's attitudes, our love for the
Lord will become their love for the Lord—expressed in gesture, prayer and song.

Chapter 7

Family Prayer

WHEN the family is assembled around the meal table—an act so symbolic of unity and love—prayer enriches the meaning of the occasion for all members of the family. For the little child, it is his best and most suitable introduction to family prayer. Besides expressing the family's unity and love, prayer at mealtime prepares a little child for the Meal of the Lord which the child will later discover at Mass.

In religious terms, the family meal is related to the many meals described in the Gospel—meals at Cana, in the house of Peter, with Matthew, in the house of Martha and Mary, with Zaccheus. There were also the many picnics which the Lord had in the desert when he was preaching to the crowds.

How often the Lord compares the Kingdom of God to a meal, to a banquet! From the very importance which Jesus has given to the meal to show his desire to be with people and to dialogue with them, Christians discover the importance of family meals. The meal should be a real sign of unity and hospitality, for in the meal Christians share the experience of friendship, joy, and reconciliation. It is why Christian parents should strive to make their family meal a real Christian experience.

The traditional thanksgiving prayer said by the father

and his blessing over the food constitute an extraordinary and powerful sign, for blessing and grace are received from the Lord through parents. Parents and children, along with their guests, can express their love for one another by extending their hands while standing around the table. Or express love and unity by singing this song:

Here we are, all together as we sing our song, joyfully.
Here we are, all together as we sing our song to the Lord.

They also might sing this song:

The love of Christ has gathered us together.
Let us rejoice in Him and be glad.
We will stand with each other,
We will stand hand in hand;

A family that prays together, stays together . . .

We will stand with each other,
We will stand hand in hand;
And together we'll spread the news
That God is in our house,
And they'll know we are Christians
By your love, by your love,
Yes, they'll know we are Christians
By your love.

In the Pentecostal season, parents and children might like
to sing this verse of the same song:

We are one in the Spirit,
We are one in the Lord;
We are one in the Spirit,
We are one in the Lord.
And we'll pray that all unity
May one day be restored,
And they'll know we are Christians
By your love, by your love,
Yes, they'll know we are Christians
By your love.

Little ones always love to share a few moments of
peace and togetherness after the evening meal. This is a
very privileged moment in family life, an opportunity to offer up the entire day, its discoveries, and the love shared by
the members of the family. Mothers in particular should be
sensitive to this specific time before they clean up the
dishes, for the little ones treasure such moments of intimacy.

There is a special evening for family prayer—Saturday
night following a day of relaxation, of joy and play together.
This family prayer, presided over by the father, could take
the following form:

First, a song in the prayer corner followed by a short
moment of silence. According to the different circumstance,
each family member can then recall joys, sorrows, difficulties, news of the neighborhood, news of the world. After
the family prays for the different intentions by joining in

prayer, by response or just by silent meditation, the small children can share their own experiences, joys, and concerns with the family.

The father or eventually a teenage brother or sister can read from the Bible, possibly a few verses of the readings for the Sunday liturgy on the next day. Finally all can join in a song or a prayer. Most often it will be the Our Father or during the month of May or October, the Hail Mary. The little ones will take this all in, cherish the experiences, and gradually learn to participate.

The Our Father is particularly beautiful in the way it has been set to music. At first, the little ones will only be able to join in for the "Hallowed be Thy Name," but they will progressively pick up the words in the restful, prayerful, and total surrendering atmosphere of family prayer. Surprisingly soon, they will know all the words and soon after will be able to join in fully.

At prayer time, the lighting of one or two candles helps children realize the solemnity of the moment as their home is lighted with the Spirit of the Lord, a spirit of love. If an older brother or sister can play the guitar, it will add to the joy of the event. While joining song to the sound of the guitar, why not lift up your hands and offer all the work, joy, and sharing of the day to the Lord?

Evening prayer, as with all family prayers, will vary. While a young child needs to repeat some usual prayers, children also need to learn spontaneous prayers when they ask for forgiveness for something that happened during the day or say a prayer of petition.

Family prayer should also include readings adapted to the day's circumstances. Some parents reflect with their children on the reading and relate it to their daily experiences, or to the events of the day as seen on television. It is an effective way to discover Christian meaning in and through the world.

When parents must leave for the evening, one of the older children can take care of the family prayer. Teenagers are both creative and serious when given the responsibility

Mothers should be sensitive to moments of intimacy...

of leading younger brothers and sisters in prayer. Parents should not check on what was done. It is important, instead, to educate children to act freely, to fulfil their responsibilities in the sight of God.

To help parents shape family prayers, many materials are available. Hymnals and records have been published providing excellent music as well as words to feed conversations with the Lord. Recorded songs also are effective when played as part of family prayer. These songs become imbedded in the consciousness of children. Often at night, children will sing snatches of such songs or they will pop out when children are happy or when they need to express their sorrow for doing wrong or to express their confidence in the Lord.

I myself have been surprised to hear my little nephews and nieces singing Christian songs and Psalms at odd moments during the day. This happens when parents have very naturally related a daily experience to Christian words, boldly actions, and songs.

A Christian family is a family that should sing often and make extensive use of religious records. Then, verses of the Psalms and biblical hymns become natural and spontaneous ways of expressing love and praise to the Lord. This prepares young children for successive steps as Christians. From the family community and liturgy they can move into the parish community and liturgy where hopefully they will add to the joyful experiences they have had at home. But it is in the home that parents start shaping the children's basic attitudes to joyful and meaningful participation in the official liturgy of the church.

Parents who have prayed together from the very beginning of their marriage and who have presented their life experiences and concerns before the Lord will very naturally extend this kind of genuine and relevant prayer to their children. If Christian parents want to educate their children into a life of prayer, they cannot be satisfied with a few routine formal prayers and good manners. Prayers should never be empty words. All life should be sung in prayers of praise.

Parents must reach a deep level in their own prayers so they can truly communicate with the Spirit who is in our hearts and who expresses Himself in truth. It is this Spirit which parents try to share with their children. But before parents can ever lead the children into the life of prayer, they need to evaluate and reconsider the quality of their own prayer.

Prayer is an intimate and personal conversation with God. There is an exchange, a dialogue. Prayer is not merely a one-sided conversation or monologue, nor is it a recitation

A family that sings together, stays together...

of stereotyped formulas. No, prayer is a true conversation with the Lord. We speak to a living person who loves us and who, through us, extends His love to every man. Like any other genuine conversation and dialogue between two people, to pray is first of all to listen to the person who speaks to us, and then to respond to him.

Real prayer is very clearly described in the Bible. The friends of God come into His presence, in a moment of silence, preparing themselves to meet with the Lord. It is always the Lord who speaks first. He takes the initiative upon which man reacts and speaks to the Lord.

We see this example in the life of Abraham, in the life of Moses, in the call of Isaiah. We see this beautifully expressed in the life of Mary. She would be the listener; she would wait for the Lord to speak to her before she would answer.

Finally, Christ shows us the example: Before He could ever speak to his Father He would go on a mountain, He would enter into silence, and in this silence the Lord His Father would speak to His heart and He could pray to His Father.

The Lord Jesus, in the most perfect way, teaches us how to speak to our Heavenly Father. He gives us His Spirit so that our prayer will come from the very depths of our own heart. Through the Lord and in the Holy Spirit, with his power and love, we can speak to God our Father. The Holy Spirit who is in our hearts teaches us to pray to the Father: "Likewise the Spirit helps us in our weakness; for we do not know how to pray as we ought, but the Spirit himself intercedes for us with sighs too deep for words" (Romans 8:26).

Chapter 8

A Child's Sunday

SUNDAY—a day of rest, leisure, hospitality, joy and love—
is above all the day of the Lord, a very special day of the
week for the entire family, but particularly for little children. At a very young age, they see Sunday as a day set
apart and the day on which they enjoy themselves most as
members of their families. It also becomes the day during
which they are gradually introduced into the worshiping
community of Christians.

Stop for a moment and see Sunday through the eyes of a
little child. It is the day when older brothers and sisters don't
have to go to school. It's a day on which father can concen-
trate on his children. It is a day on which mother and father
have the chance to interact, to talk things over, to express
before their children mutual love through gesture, through
word, through warm presence.

Sunday is special, even in the clothes that all members
of the family, including little children, wear. The clothes
which are more "dressed up" than everyday clothes an-
nounce that it is a day of feasting and rejoicing. Sunday is
the day when mother cooks a special meal and the table is
special, too, decorated with flowers or possibly candlelight.
The day is also special in regard to people: the entire family
is gathered around the table. Sunday is a day of reconciliation, a day of rediscovering one another.

Sunday is a day for celebrating life through joy, through singing, through recreation, a day for sharing, a play day. On Sunday, a father can spend time with his children, taking them out for a walk, a ride in the car, a visit to the zoo or to the park. The young child is very sensitive to these little signs of Sunday, to the atmosphere of relaxation, joy, and sharing which he experiences in his family on the Lord's Day.

Sunday is a day to let our minds rest contemplatively on the rose in bud, on the child at play, on a tree in full bloom —and on the love that makes our family one. In these silent and receptive moments, parents and children reach an awareness of the divine creativity that holds the group together. They become aware of the divine love reflected in

More "dressed up" than everyday clothes...

their family life together. This love and creativity deserve
to be celebrated, and God has put one day aside to celebrate life, to celebrate love.

When celebrating Sunday with their children, parents
affirm the meaningfulness of the world and mankind. Together, they experience the world and their family in an aspect other than the everyday one. In celebrating Sunday, a
family experiences union, tranquility, contemplation, tuning
itself into life, joy and peace.

This power to celebrate and to achieve leisure is one of
the fundamental powers of man. Only man has the power to
overstep the boundaries of the everyday world and reach
out to superhuman life-giving forces that refresh and renew
him before he turns back to his daily routine. Sunday is par
excellence the day of awareness of the divine principles
which dwell within the world and within the heart of every
man. To celebrate the first day, a day set aside from work,
gives man the opportunity to become aware of the real mystery of his life, of the progressive process of civilization in
which he is engaged with Christ.

God's precept of the sabbatical rest is to be understood
by parents as designed to humanize and ultimately to "di-
vinize" our life. God does not only recommend leisure and
relaxation, but he sanctifies it. God knows that through leisure we renew our relationship with others, with the world,
and, ultimately, with God himself. Through Sundays, and
its times of leisure and family relaxation, family life and
spirit develop.

Thus speaks the prophet Isaiah (58:13-14): "If you
hold from traveling on Sabbath, from following your own
pursuits on my holy day, if you call the Sabbath a delight
and the Lord's day honorable, if you honor it by not following your own ways, seeking your own interests, or speaking
with malice, then you shall delight in the Lord, and I will
make you ride on the heights of the earth."

If parents are attentive on Sunday to their children,
they will very naturally be attentive to the presence of
God's Law in their family, in their hearts and in the lives of

their own children. This is why Christian parents will see
to it that the atmosphere of the home on Sunday is quite
different from the atmosphere of the home during the week.

To illustrate the way the all-important atmosphere of
peace, leisure and joy becomes part of family life on Sunday, I can cite various examples. In each instance, the
family is responding in its own way to celebration of the
Lord's Day. In one large family of seven children, the spirit of the Sabbath celebration is consciously sought from
Saturday evening until Monday morning. Parents and children together make a special effort to banish all discord and
disputes, and household tasks are done cooperatively. The
day is highlighted by something special which has been
planned in advance: a visit to grandparents, to the country,
to a local event.

Divine love reflected in a family together on Sunday . . .

In another family, Sunday breakfast is taken in common—everybody is there to share the meal in joy and peace. During breakfast and before going to church, one member of the family selects and plays church music and songs on the hi-fi. The music adds a special quality and reminds the family of the divine presence in the home. The music can be chosen from classical works, from folk songs, or from contemporary church music. This prepares those who go to church to enter into the spirit of the liturgy. The little ones who stay at home discover that Sunday morning is something special: it is filled with songs, with music, with joy.

Some families prepare for the Lord's Day with a special prayer on Saturday evening and with readings from the New Testament selections to be heard at Mass the next day. If there are children who are old enough, one of them can prepare the reading. Adults are surprised to see how seriously a 10- or 12-year-old boy or girl prepares for this reading. The Saturday evening prayer could start with the singing of a hymn or psalm. Then everybody could sit down for the reading, followed by family singing. The ending can be an appropriate hymn or psalm the children learn at school or at church. During the penitential times of the year or if some dramatic event has happened in the world, the prayer could be ended by a penitential litany asking God's help, forgiveness, and mercy for those who have suffered during the week.

In another family, on Sunday morning the candle before the picture of the Risen Lord is lighted. This simple gesture of celebrating the Resurrection of the Lord is a powerful reminder of the great mystery of our own resurrection it is shared by the entire family. This candle is also a sign and symbol of the presence of the Risen Lord in the midst of the family, for as the Lord says, "Where two or three are gathered in My Name, there I am in the midst of them."

There is no better way of celebrating the union and love of the family than by sharing the same meal, by giving

thanks to the Lord for this joy of communion, of family re-
union. Thanksgiving can be expressed through a communal
song or prayer before Sunday dinner. The song can express
the resurrection as in a triumphant alleluia, or it could be
the verse of a psalm—the 96th, for instance, which is set
to beautiful music in the Hymnal for Young Christians
copyright F.E.L. Church Publications, Ltd., Chicago, (p. 82).
The words sing out:

This is the day that the Lord has made;
Let us be glad and rejoice.
Halleluia, halleluia, halleluia.

Sunday breakfast a time of joy and peace...

In the Hymnal (p. 46) there is an affirmative *gloria*:

Glory to God, glory, oh praise Him, alleluia!
Glory to God, glory, oh praise the name of the Lord.

To express the joy of being together the family can hold
hands, with small children extending little hands to brothers
and sisters, to father and mother, while joining in song
as best they can. The Hymnal (p. 45) offers the following:

Here we are all together as we sing our song joyfully.
Here we are, all together,
As we pray we'll always be.

During the Pentecostal season, the family can sing (p. 71):

We are one in the Spirit,
We are one in the Lord;
We are one in the Spirit,
We are one in the Lord.
And we pray that unity
May one day be restored.

This first part should be intoned by the one who sings it,
then everyone in the family can join in:

And they'll know we are Christians
   By our love, by our love;
Yes, they'll know we are Christians
   By our love.

For the Sundays after Easter, the Hymnal has an appropriate chorus (p. 69) to start the family meal:

Allelu! Allelu! Everybody sing Allelu!
For the Lord has risen it is true.
Everybody sing Allelu!

For Christians, this Resurrection theme should be dominant on each and every Sunday. It has been this way al-

ways, a fact important to recall in contemporary awareness of what the Lord's Day is all about. The first generations of Christians celebrated each Sunday as the anniversary day of the Resurrection of the Lord. Sunday, the first day of the week, the day of the Sun, was the day on which pagans would adore and celebrate the sun; Christians replaced the celebration of the sun with the celebration of the Lord's Resurrection. This is the day Christians celebrate the victory of life over death, this new strength, this new life given to men.

During the early decades of Christian times, Judaeo-Christians would join the Jews on the Sabbath in the synagogues and refrain from work. But on the next day they would celebrate the Resurrection of the Lord through the Eucharist, by which the real celebration of the Resurrection

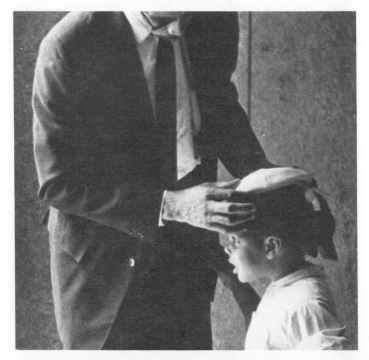

Dressed for the Sunday celebration ...

takes place. Only later, when Christianity was officially accepted by the State, did Sunday become a day of rest.

It is the weekly celebration of the Resurrection which
makes Sunday a festival in which a certain time is set apart
and consecrated for the divinization of man through the
Resurrection, through the Eucharist. Each Sunday, Christians all over the world gather to celebrate the feast in honor
of the Lord. Each Sunday, Christians celebrate their own
mystery—the mystery of their own resurrection in the Lord.
Each Sunday, Christians celebrate rebirth to a new life
which God gives us now and the fullness of life which he
promises us in the future. Thus speaks the Lord, our God, to
his people: "Come to my feast. Come to my banquet. Come
and celebrate with My Son a new and eternal life which is
yours."

Little children are too young to join in the celebration
of the Eucharist, but what they experience will have a lasting effect. The attitude which their parents have toward
the celebration of the Eucharist constitutes an important
part of a small child's religious education. Unfortunately, for
too many parents the Eucharist is only a gesture of obedi-
ence to the Lord, a fidelity to family tradition, the proof of
good will towards God. Some go to church dragging their
feet. They leave behind a bad impression on little children.

Parents should return from church with the glad tidings
of what happened and of what was said. This can be done
at meal time when parents use the songs and prayers of
the Sunday Mass at the meal table. The parents can also
pray for the same intentions at home as in church. In all
this, parents are breaking the bread of the Word for their
little children. Whatever a parent does for his child, he is
also doing for the Lord.

Where little children accompany parents to church,
parents should make sure they see everything that goes on.
This makes it important to sit up front, close to the altar
and the priest. Parents should join joyfully in the singing, for
this has a strong influence on children. There is no better
way for children to be introduced to liturgical prayer or

worship than by being with their parents at a time of deep and sincere prayer. When parents hold back from participating in the worship of the community, they will have a difficult time helping their children to discover the joy of celebrating the Lord's Day in His House. This early experience is a point at which children begin preparing for the seemingly-distant day of their own First Communion.

Parents are priests to their children. Parents are prophets to their children. Parents are shepherds to their children. This is the threefold mission entrusted to husband and wife on the day of their marriage—in anticipation of the day they will be father and mother.

What happens on Sunday for all Christians, small and big, young and old, is summed up in Exodus (20:9) and its message can be adapted to the role of parents and children on the Lord's Day.

"Remember to celebrate the day of the Lord. From Monday to Saturday you will do all your work, but Sunday is a special day for God. It is the day of the Lord. You shall do no hard work this day; neither your father nor your mother, nor any one else who lives with you. It took God six days to make Heaven and Earth and the Sea and all that

Parents should join joyfully in the singing . . .

walks on the land and swims in the sea. On Sunday God finished his work and He rested in order to see how beautiful all his works really were. That is why the Lord has made Sunday a very special day for us, to rejoice and to celebrate with us."

Participation influences little children . . .

Chapter 9

A Child's Christmas

CHRISTMAS the world over is a children's festival, a child's celebration, the climax of the most wonderful and exciting season of the year. And it should be a climax, coming after four weeks of family and liturgical preparation, for it marks the incomparable coming of the Lord into the world.

Preparations during the Advent season enable the family to express hope, expectation, and desire for this coming of the Lord that He might fill hearts with joy and light, that He might bring love and peace to the world. But Advent is not so much something to *explain* to children as something to *experience* with them.

The theme of Advent is expressed beautifully in the closing verses of the Book of Revelation (Apocalypse) of St. John:

" 'Surely I am coming soon'. Amen.
Come, Lord Jesus."

Advent means coming. Is there anything closer to the child's experience in language than these words, "I am coming?" The season of Advent reminds us powerfully that Jesus, who came in history, who continues to come in mystery, is finally to come in majesty. Christians are yearning, calling to the Lord. The spirit in our hearts says, "Come and heal all divided hearts, all divisions among nations. Make all things right." The Christian, with all the vigor of his being, expresses his desire to see Christ fill the heart of every man with his love and power so that peace and unity may one day be restored among nations. For children, Advent should express Christian faith, hope and charity in family prayer, song, and activity.

The first family activity is the making of an Advent tree. Because this tradition is so symbolic, it is successful with little children. My preference is the table wreath, which can be hung from the ceiling. The meaning of the wreath is clear: The circular form is a symbol of eternity; God has no beginning and no end. The evergreen is a symbol of everlasting life, the life Christ brings to the world. The candles are symbols of the everlasting conquest by the light of the world, which is Christ, over the darkness of sin.

During the first week of Advent, at dinnertime, when

Christmas the world over is a children's festival...

all are gathered together, one member of the family has the privilege of lighting the first candle. As the weeks go by, each child takes turns. During the second week of Advent, two candles are lighted, during the third week, three, and on the fourth Sunday before Christmas four. This progression of light shows the progression of Christ's presence and dwelling in the world.

While lighting the candles, the family can sing a song to Christ, the light of the world. During this season, grace before meals can be special and closer to the liturgy of the Church. As the candles are lighted, one family member could intone, for instance, the following:

> (*The leader of the song starts*)
> Sing your praise to Christ,
>   The light of the living God.
> (*All the family answers*)
> Glory to you, oh Lord.
> Sing your praise to Christ,
>   The son of the living God.
> Glory to you, oh Lord.

Next, the father of the family can read a short prayer adapted from the Advent Liturgy.

Advent also is a time for preparing gifts, something little children love to do. Children also need to realize that the most beautiful gift to Jesus is an open and loving heart. Advent is a time for children to say Yes to the Lord, to say Yes to their parents, to say Yes to brothers and sisters. For Advent is a real time of conversion, of coming back to the Lord as our God.

To symbolize the daily Yes to the Lord, one family I know celebrates the Christmas novena beginning on December 16 by taking the Christmas crib down from the attic. The crib is displayed on a table in the living room with only two figures placed alongside—Mary and Joseph—to await the coming of the Lord. The manger is left empty and each child is given a little lamb which represents himself. The lambs are placed at equal distances from the crib. Every night at prayer time, the parents have their evening prayer with the children before the crib. It starts by lighting a candle, as they sing:

Sing your praise to Christ,
The light of the living God.
Glory to you, oh Lord.

The Advent family prayer generally consists of one Hail Mary and a litany adapted to the children's daily life. Through this litany, the child will progressively discover the special penitential prayer and spirit which he shares with the Church during this Advent season. He will discover that Christians put all their trust in the Lord. The litany could run as follows:

Father or Mother say: "We love the Lord with all our hearts; Lord, hear our prayer."

All can respond by saying, "Lord, come and help us," or else sing: "Lord Jesus, come. Lord, give us help. Lord, give us love."

Parents: "That we may always share our toys with brothers and sisters, we pray to you, O Lord."

All respond, using the same answer as the first time.

Parents: "That we may always be kind to our mother and father, we pray to you, O Lord. That we may always say Yes to what the Lord asks us to do, that we may always say Yes to what our parents ask us to do."

Response as before.

Then the children can be invited to make their own petition to the Lord. To help children reflect on their day, parents can mention some good things done by the children, such as sharing crayons with a playmate. The child might then say: "Lord, I shared my crayons with Cindy today. Thank you, Lord." For each of these, the family can respond with "We give you thanks, O Lord our Savior." Advent family prayer generally ends with an Advent hymn such as "Rejoice, rejoice, oh Israel." When the prayer is finished, the child then takes his little lamb and moves it slightly forward toward the crib, symbolizing the way we move closer to Jesus the more we love.

Sometimes, parents will be inclined not to have a song in Advent because a child misbehaved. Symbolically, as a punishment, the lamb would get no closer to the crib. This would have a severe effect on the children and parents should be extremely careful—and hesitant—about using such a symbolic punishment. Parents should not use a child's love for Jesus to help keep discipline in the home. Such phrases as the following ought to be banished from family vocabularies: "Today, Jesus is not happy at all with you, Johnny, because you did this or that." Or, "God is very sad, Johnny, because—"

It can be difficult for parents to refrain from calling upon the name of the Lord to help keep discipline or reinforce parental authority, but, religiously speaking, doing so can be extremely harmful to the child. He might, through such experiences, have a complete distortion of the image of God, who is a loving father, a forgiving father. It is important for children to realize that both parents and God have constant love for him. The child who has done wrong needs to have the complete security that he can come back to his parents and find forgiveness, and that they will help him open his heart to others and change.

During the novena before Christmas, the home can be decorated with collages and drawings, done by the older children. Little children can share in the joy and creativity by watching and also by helping with some glue or by adding a little color here and there.

The symbolic creative art could have the following themes:

O Shepherd of Israel, You who guide Your holy people, oh come redeem us by Your mighty arm.

O wisdom that comes forth from the mouth of the Most High, You who are foretold by many prophets, oh come and show us the way that leads us to our heavenly home.

O David's son, oh shield of peoples and kings, the
whole world calls upon You. Oh come, make us free.

O key of David, oh scepter of Israel's house, You who
reign upon creation; come to set us free, those who
wander about in darkness.

O rising sun, oh splendor of everlasting light, oh
come and shed Your light on those who live in the
night of death.

O king of all people, You who make all nations one, oh
come to free mankind which You have made.

O Immanuel, You are the king and hope of all nations.
Redeemer of all people, oh come and save us.

In many homes, the children prepare a gift for someone who otherwise would not receive one. Once again, parents should encourage their children to give a gift which
they make on their own or to give one of their treasured
toys. What is important is not the material value of the gift,
but the generosity expressed in the giving.

Meanwhile, using the Advent tree, the family has the
opportunity on the eighth of December, the Feast of the Im-
maculate Conception, to describe to little children the role
played by Mary in the coming of the Lord. For illustration,
parents can select a reproduction from the marvelous paintings of Mary, such as the one by Fra Angelico. There are
several of the Annunication. In order to center attention on
Mary, a picture of her alone is preferable for this particular
occasion. The picture can be placed close to the Advent
wreath so that the candlelight will shine on it, conveying
the feeling that Mary is waiting for the light of the world
to be drawn from her.

It is important to show Mary's role in God's plan of salvation. She is that woman who has said Yes to the Lord, becoming the blessed mother of God our Savior. Parents must

relate Mary to the redemption received through her son
Jesus. As the mother of God, she cannot be separated from
the Church which is the continuation of Christ here on
earth. Because Mary was called in the great simplicity of
her ordinary life to collaborate in the plan of salvation of
God, parents should keep this simplicity and avoid idealized
presentations of Mary. The more concrete the better. Parents should situate Mary in her country as a woman belonging to people, the people of Israel; a woman like many other women in the village where she lived; a woman who was
chosen by God to become the mother of his Son. It can be
told like this to little children:

Many, many years ago in a city called Nazareth,
there lived a young girl named Mary. She was just like
all the other women in the country of Palestine. She often
went to the well to get water for her family. She made
the dough and baked the bread. She even made clothing.
Sometimes she went to the river to wash clothes. Yes, she
tried to do all that she could to keep her home nice. And
she did this with a lot of love for God and for her neigh-
bors. People in the city loved Mary. When she went
through the streets she would stop to chat with them. But
Mary also liked to spend a little time in her room just to
be there by herself and with the Lord, for she knew
that the Lord her God was always with her. She, like
many people in her country, also prayed to God, saying,
"Lord, send us a saviour; Lord, come to save our people."
God knew what was deep in the heart of Mary. He knew
Mary always answered yes to whatever he asked from
her. God prepared this young girl to become the mother
of His only Son Jesus.

Now, let me take the Bible and see what happened
long ago in that little city called Nazareth to a girl named
Mary. She was in her room and a messenger of the Lord
was sent to her. God was sending Mary great news. At
first, Mary was a little afraid of the angel coming into
her home, but the angel said to her, "Do not be afraid,

Mary. I have come to tell you great news." The angel said to her, "Hail Mary, full of grace, the Lord is with you." Mary was a little surprised at hearing those beautiful words spoken to her. Then the angel told her the great news: "You are to become the mother of a child. This child will be called Jesus. He will be the Son of God and he will be a great king forever." Then Mary answered: "How shall this be possible?" The angel answered: "Nothing is impossible to the Lord. He will take care of you and protect you." Mary said to the angel: "I am the servant of the Lord. May His will be done." And the angel left.

Here, father or mother can comment on the attitude of Mary. She is silent. She is attentive to the word of God, which she knows well. For a long time, the people of Abraham and Moses were waiting for a Savior. Mary understood the great secret of God and she kept the secret deep in her heart.

As Christmas gets closer, the Advent days of song, prayer and family activity will begin to bear fruit in understanding and appreciation of what is to take place. Now, too, gifts begin to play a prominent part in the preparations for Christmas. Parents should explain the why of gift-giving:

When Christians give gifts to one another, they like to celebrate, to remember the greatest gift God made to us on Christmas Day. God loves us so much He gave us His only Son, Jesus. Jesus is the greatest gift we ever could imagine, for it is through Jesus that we receive God's life in us. Jesus shows us, therefore, how to love God our Father, and how to love one another.

Our joy in Christmas is very great and we want to show that love is in our hearts. Love helps us to share; love helps us to be joyful with one another. That's why we like to show our love for others by making gifts, not only for those who are in our home, but also for those who are sick. On Christmas Day, every person should feel loved by God and by people, for Christmas is the celebration of

God's love among men. God is with us. Love is now in the world.

Gifts and Christmas shopping unavoidably lead to the question of Santa Claus. To questions about whether there is really a Santa Claus, one useful rule must be recalled: avoid lying to children when they ask questions. In the case of Santa Claus, it is not desirable to mix up belief in him with belief in the coming of Jesus, the Son of God. It would be preferable if children did not believe in Santa Claus. He certainly should not be the center of this Christian feast.

When children are confronted with Santa Claus everywhere—from the TV screen to the department store—it makes sense to answer children's questions by saying: "Santa Claus is a man who helps people find out what kind of gifts they want. That's his job and he must get very tired working all day. Yes, there are many different Santas—on street corners, in department stores. They enjoy making children happy and finding out what they want for Christmas. There are wonderful stories about Santa Claus, about his home in the North Pole and his lovable reindeer. But these are stories that we like to hear, like the make-believe stories we make up sometimes."

In preparing the crib and manger, parents can unfold the Christmas story and its importance to Christians. Little children can be told how the crèche recalls for the family what happened 2,000 years ago in a stable in Bethlehem. Parents can point out the way each figure in the manger approaches the crib in a prayerful attitude:

Mary and Joseph kneel down before Baby Jesus. They adore Him, for this little baby is the Son of God. Shepherds who kept their sheep during the night were told the good news by angels. They were told to go to the crib. They were told by the angels that the Lord, the Son of God, was born and they would find Him lying in the crib, a little child. The shepherds were the first to see the little Jesus. What did they do? They saw a baby and they felt there was something very special about this baby. They knelt down and adored him. (Parents here should point out the reverential attitude of the shepherds). They realized how great the news was and they went to tell the good news to their friends. They said to their friends: "A child is born to us, he is lying in a manger, he is poor. He is the Lord, he is the Son of God. It is He who brings peace and love to all of us."

Every year at Christmas we like to celebrate this joy for Mary, for Joseph, for the great joy of the shepherds, and for the great joy of every man who believes in Jesus, who believes that Jesus is truly the Son of God. But every year Jesus doesn't become a baby again. What we celebrate is the birthday of the Lord Jesus. His birthday is so important that we get ready for it with great joy.

When people love one another, Jesus is there. Jesus grows more and more in the hearts of people who try to make peace, to forgive, to love one another. At Christmas, Jesus is in the city, in the streets; He is more and more with those families who celebrate His coming in their homes. He is wherever people love one another, where people try to make others happy.

The Lord Jesus was a little child, just like you. He needed to be taken care of by a mother. Here we see Mary. Joseph also would look after Jesus and he would look after Mary. The crib also shows that Jesus, who is the Son of God, was born in a stable instead of being born in a comfortable home in a warm bed. He was born like a very, very poor child. That's why Jesus is so close to the heart of the poor, to those who have no home, to those who have little food. That's why Jesus wants us also to do something on Christmas for the poor.

Christian parents also have the chance to explain the meaning of candles at Christmas. While arranging the candles, a parent can point out:

We use candles in our family for a birthday party. We celebrate a birthday by lighting candles. This tells a person how much we like him, how important he is to us, how happy we are to have him with us. Jesus has been with us many, many years. When a mother and father love one another, Jesus is with them; Jesus lives with that family; Jesus lives in their hearts. We want Jesus to stay with us. He shall always be with us in our hearts and in our homes. That's why we like to celebrate His birthday. That's why we light candles. They give light in a home; they give joy to our hearts. Let's light a candle. Look at this candle: it helps us think of Jesus. God our heavenly Father is pleased when He sees that we open our hearts to Jesus, that we ask Him to help us love people. God our Father sees how hard we try to make people happy at Christmas and he is pleased. God loves to see our eyes and our faces filled with light and joy, because God wants everybody to be happy.

Let's light another candle. This candle shows us that Jesus is a light; He makes us happy. He also teaches us how to make others happy. Sometimes I say to myself, or I say to your father, our little son Johnny is really a great joy and a great light in our lives.

Your mother and your daddy are also a great light and a great joy to you. Why? Because of Jesus, who lives in our hearts. Because of Jesus we have this great love and this great joy we can share with you. Jesus is our light. Jesus gives everyone in the world His joy, His peace, His love. That's why so many people celebrate Christmas with lots of candles and lots of lights. Wherever people open their hearts to Jesus there is light and joy. Shall we try to find out the many places in our neighborhood where people turn on lights to celebrate the birthday of Jesus? Maybe you would like to thank Jesus for bringing His joy and His light into our home. I know a song full of light and joy. Listen.

Christ the light of the living God.
Glory to God, Glory. All praise him,
Alleluia. Glory to God, Glory. All praise
the name of the Lord.

Christmas Eve itself presents a special opportunity for including little children in a family liturgical celebration. This can be built around the final arranging of the crêche. A family procession can take place with both parents and children carrying candles to the manger. There Jesus can be placed in the crib in a special ceremony. (A detailed description of such a celebration appears at the end of this book. Appendix 1)

The fitting close to the Christmas season is the feast of Epiphany on January 6. This is a real children's festival. Indeed, the Christmas story would be incomplete without an account of the mysterious star that guided the Wise Men of the East to a stable in Bethlehem.

One or two days before the feast day, children can prepare crowns to wear in acting out the parts of the three kings. The crowns can be made out of cardboard and covered with colored paper. They can be made by the boys. Stars also can be cut out and pasted on sticks. The girls can help to make cakes — the kings' cakes. Insert three special objects in the dough—such as a pea, a piece of apple or carrot and a bean. Whoever gets one of the three special objects in his piece of cake becomes one of the kings. When an older child gets such an object, he has the chance to turn it over to a smaller brother or sister so he or she can play the role of king.

The crowning should be done with solemnity by the father of the family. It is incredible how special and attentive the eating of the cake can be on such an occasion—followed by the enthusiasm for the crowning.

Now all is ready for the procession. The "star" carriers and the "kings" (each carrying a statue of his king) proceed toward the manger. Those carrying the stars symbolize the way the Wise Men found their way to Bethlehem. All assemble around the creche. The statues of the kings are placed near the crib. The family then sits around the creche and a carol is sung about the kings coming to adore Jesus. Then there is a reading of the Gospel story of the adoration

of the kings. This should be read by a parent or an older
brother or sister.

Parents can converse with their children about the reading so that the children can tell them once again what happened in Judea, in Jerusalem, and in Bethlehem. Parents can
tell their children the meaning of the Gospel reading:

Christ has come not only to save His people, the Jewish people, but He has come to save all people. He has
been recognized by the kings from the Far East, kings
who have come from very far away, from other nations.
Yes, it is often so. Christ shall be adored and worshiped
by those nations that are still pagan. He shall be accepted by some. Those kings shall adore Him and fall on
their knees. Others will feel threatened by this new king
of Israel, by this new kingdom He's coming to establish.

From this reading, the family can turn to prayers of
petition. The family can ask the Lord to make himself
known as the King of all nations to those who still haven't
heard of Him. Father or mother can introduce the prayer
by saying:

With our heart, let us pray. Oh Lord, have mercy, hear
our prayer.

Everyone answers:

Oh Lord, have mercy. Hear our prayer.

*One of the older children or a parent can lead the prayer
of petitions:*

Lord, may the people of all the earth get to know You
and gather in Your Kingdom, we pray to the Lord. Oh
Lord, hear our prayer.

Everyone answers:

Oh Lord, have mercy. Hear our prayer.

Again the leader of the prayer:

Let Christians everywhere in the world show the good

news of the Kingdom of Heaven which Christ comes to establish. We pray to the Lord.

Everyone:

Oh Lord, have mercy. Hear our prayer.

Leader:

Let each member of our family accept Christ in his heart as being the King of his life, the One to whom we offer everything.

Everyone:

Oh Lord, have mercy. Hear our prayer.

Leader:

Lord, on this day You have used a star to show Your Only Begotten Son to the nations of the world. Grant that we who know You may one day meet You face to face in Your Heavenly Majesty, through the Lord Jesus Christ and through the spirit who lives in our hearts.

Everybody answers:

Amen.

At the end of this prayer, the family can either sing a Christmas carol which expresses the story of the Magi coming to adore Christ or else a familiar carol from the Christmas season.

And so a child's Christmas comes to an end as he passes another year in his growth as a Christian.

Chapter 10

The Meaning of Lent and Easter

*T*HE season of Lent is a time for the entire family to be more attentive to the words of Jesus and a time to try harder to put His teachings into practice. With this in mind, parents can prepare their children to respond to the conditions Jesus sets for those who want to enter the Kingdom of Heaven.

Lent is, thereby, a journey of 40 days with Jesus on the way to Jerusalem. It is a road which parents and their children take, realizing that it is not an easy trip. For, as Jesus said to his followers, to follow Him is to take up your daily cross. To join in the celebration of the death and resurrection of the Lord, Christians must stretch out their arms to each other and to the love of God.

During Lent, parents have the chance to bring home the words of Jesus and to connect them with attitudes and actions. To have children remember the words of Jesus write them on a large piece of paper and tack them up on the wall of the prayer corner in the living room. The wording can follow the pattern of the Beatitudes and can apply to the family situation: Happy is the child who is always willing to forgive, for he shall always be forgiven. Happy is the child who always says the truth. Happy is the child who freely gives or shares.

Jesus is with us through the cross...

Along with these words, which will accumulate as Lent progresses, specific efforts to apply them can be urged. It is better child psychology to propose one specific action or attitude for the week and another for the following week—instead of asking children to make *all* efforts in the same week. One week parents can stress helping people. The words of Jesus to put on the scroll could be: Happy is the child who tries to help people and make them happy. At the time of Saturday evening prayer, parents can discuss concrete ways to put this in practice. For instance; Happy is the child who helps father take out the garbage. Happy is the child who helps a brother or sister put his room in order. Happy is the child who helps his brother put away his toys. To make things more concrete, children can be encouraged to draw the things they decide to do, or to draw those events through which they can bring the good news of Jesus into their home, into their neighborhood. Such drawings are the personal treasure of the children and are to be displayed in their room.

This 40-day journey will lead to the day of Jesus' triumphant entry into Jerusalem on Palm Sunday. If there is a procession, be sure to take the children. To prepare them, tell the children the Gospel narrative which can be found in the blessing of the Palms just before the Palm Sunday Mass; or else in Matthew (21:1-9). Parents also might like to play records and sing Psalm 23 with their children. This psalm is sung during the procession. In the Hymnal for Young Christians, page 60, the words are put to the rhythm of an Israeli folksong. The rhythm calls for clapping of hands, which appeals so much to little children. If a child does not go to a palm procession, parents can still bring back the palms and read a very simple adaptation of Jesus' triumphant entry into Jerusalem. It can begin this way:

Jesus is someone we love very much. Jesus is someone who tells us how to become His friend. Jesus is our King. We sing His praise, for He gives us His great victory over evil and death. Listen to what happened to Jesus the day

He entered Jerusalem. (The text of Jesus' triumphant entry into Jerusalem could be inserted here. Matthew 11:1-9)

A few days after Palm Sunday, Christians celebrate the Last Supper, when Christ gave His great commandment of love: Love one another as I love you. He did this just after He washed the feet of His disciples. The lesson is clear: he who wants to be a follower of Jesus has to be a servant of his fellowman.

Holy Thursday calls for a special dinner, similar to the Jewish Passover meal, for Christ sent his disciples to Jerusalem in order to prepare for such a meal. Before sharing this meal, the father can read aloud the narrative of the Last Supper and Jesus' commandment of brotherly love in Luke (22:7-13). After supper, the section of John's Gospel on the washing of the disciples' feet can be read. This gesture will baffle little children, but it can be explained in the following way:

Long ago, in hot countries like Jerusalem, people walked a lot and their feet became covered with dust. So when friends came into a house a servant washed their feet before they came into the living room or into the dining room. This was always done by servants. Jesus did the washing to show how we must be ready to serve other people, to be ready to help others.

Today we have other ways to show we are helpful. In our family, we don't have to wash the feet of one another any more because this is no longer done. But we can be servants in many different ways. For instance, we can do what Jesus did when we help clear the table after dinner. We wash feet and are servants when we put our toys back and clean up a mess in our room. Or we can clean and polish shoes for our brothers and sisters.

In approaching Good Friday, parents should be careful not to emphasize the painful details of the crucifixion,—the nails, the thorns, the spear, the blood and the thirst. Instead, parents should dwell on the desire of Christ to stretch His own arms, to stretch and share His own life with everyone, starting with the thief who is crucified next to Him. To the thief, the Lord said: "Tonight you will be with me in the Kingdom of Heaven." What should be stressed is Christ's attitude of total self-surrender, of great Amen, which the Lord said to His Father. He personifies complete lack of selfishness, complete openness to others.

If the family doesn't go to the liturgy of Good Friday in the parish, the evening prayer can be a miniature of the celebration of the Cross held in church. It is important to underline the two aspects of the Mystery of the Cross: the aspect of death, of solitude, but also the aspect of victory, of glory. In putting the Cross in a place of honor, parents can use a simple cross of wood or a cross on which Christ extending his arms toward all helps a child to understand that Jesus came to teach us to say yes to one another. The cross should have signs of glory and victory around it—flowers, candles, a golden background.

In family prayer on Good Friday, it is important to point out that Jesus is with us through the cross, that Jesus has freed us from death: Jesus is alive, alleluia. Jesus shares his life with us, alleluia. Jesus shares his light with us, alleluia. A song evoking this victory over sin and death achieved by Christ through his resurrection could fittingly close Good Friday home prayer. There is a traditional hymn in the People's Hymnal, "Behold the royal cross on high" and similar songs in other hymnals.

After the 40 days of preparation, Christians reach the key point of the liturgical year: the Christian mystery which is the resurrection of the Lord. It is Easter, the great feast of the year, of Jesus' birth to a new and everlasting life. It is the mystery through which man has found a new hope, a new future.

Christmas would be without meaning if it did not lead us toward Easter. Bethlehem only receives meaning from Jerusalem. Strangely enough, our family traditions and celebrations show that we still have a long way to go to restore

Easter to its true importance, though Christians do, in fact, celebrate Easter every Sunday. Every Sunday the Christian community celebrates the day of the Lord, which is the day of Christ's resurrection.

Easter calls for a special celebration of the resurrection. It is the time for parents to point out the signs of new life in nature. Spring explodes all around the little child. The trees—seemingly dead for many months—bud and blossom with life. The air fills with the sound of birds; meadows are decked with daffodils; public gardens are colored with tulips and crocuses. How natural, then, for parents to relate the experience of this new life bursting around them to the new life which Christ gives through His resurrection. For the Christian, the signs of this new life in nature are signs of the alleluias which are bursting forth in homes and churches. Jesus is alive, alleluia. These natural signs are linked to liturgical signs. At Easter, flowers can decorate the family room, the crucifix, or even better, an art reproduction of the Risen Lord, the Lord in Glory.

Songs also are important for the child to realize it is Easter. A joyful alleluia could start or end the family prayer.

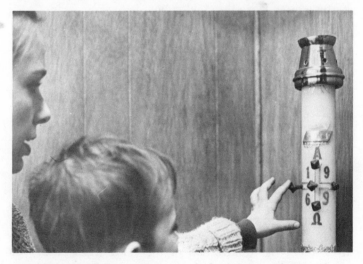

The Paschal candle is symbol of Risen Christ...

An alleluia or some Easter anthem can be the prayer before
meals. Or else, songs which celebrate the coming of new life
which is given through the resurrection. Examples are available in the Deiss Hymnal—Psalm 100, on page 72; Psalm
65, on page 88. The word alleluia has almost magical effect
on children and so it should be seen as well as heard. Alleluia should be represented in some way on the walls of the
dining or living room.

In addition, candles and light play an important role.
Light symbolizes life. The Paschal candle which is lit during
the Paschal vigil in the church symbolizes the Risen
Lord who now shares His life with us. During Easter week, a
visit can be made to the church in order to see the Paschal
candle. At home, a special candle can be the Paschal candle around which family prayer takes place. The Paschal
candle can light the small candle each child holds in his
hand. Parents need to explain the symbolism of the Paschal
candle—the unending love, the unending light through which
we can light our own lives and through which we can revivi-
fy our own love.

The following songs are suited to family prayer in the
Easter season. Have the children join in to sing alleluia:

We were darkness in sin, alleluia;
And now we are light in Christ, alleluia.
So let your light shine through the world, alleluia.
Alleluia.

Jesus is risen today, alleluia.
And we are risen with Christ, alleluia.
So let your light shine through the world, alleluia.
Alleluia.

On Easter day and throughout Easter week, parents can
help children discover more about Jesus, the risen Lord, by
reading at evening prayer one of the many Gospel narratives about the resurrection of the Lord. These texts will
need some adaptation for children. But in relating them par-

ents are following the example of Christ in presenting the core of the Christian message: the resurrection of the Lord. Here are appropriate Gospel narratives for family reading:

On Easter Sunday, Mark 16:1-8: Jesus appears to Mary Magdalene and to Mary the mother of James.

On Easter Monday, Luke 24:13-35: Jesus appears to the disciples at Emmaus.

On Easter Tuesday, Luke 24:36-47: Jesus appears to his disciples in Jerusalem.

On Easter Wednesday, John 21:1-14: Jesus appears to his disciples by the Sea of Tiberias.

On Easter Thursday, John 20:11-18: Jesus appears to Mary Magdalene.

On Easter Friday, Matthew 28:16-20: Jesus appears to his disciples in Galilee.

On Easter Saturday, John 20:1-9: Jesus appears to Peter and John.

On the first Sunday after Easter, there is the final report in John 20:19-31. Jesus appears to his disciples and gives them the order to go throughout the world and forgive those who come and ask pardon of the Lord.

Fifty days after Easter, Pentecost is celebrated, the coming of the Spirit upon the Apostles, so that they can continue the mission of Christ. Parents and teachers must be careful not to insist upon the extraordinary phenomena which go along with the outpouring of the Spirit: the tongues of fire, the dove, the thunder. Instead emphasize that the Lord keeps His promise: "I shall be with you till the end of time." "I will send you the Holy Spirit." The Holy Spirit is the spirit of love, life, truth, physical strength. Jesus' friends will no longer keep the good news of Jesus' death and resurrection to themselves. They will be pushed by the Spirit to go into public places and proclaim that Christ whom they had put to death is now risen.

In speaking of the Father, the Son, and the Holy Spirit to young children, parents should focus on the Trinity's relationship to us and the divine relationship to one another in terms of actions. The Holy Spirit can be spoken of it terms which express dynamic action in the following ways:

The Holy Spirit is someone who helps us do the work of Jesus. He is someone who helps us find the right words to speak to the Lord, to find the right things to do for people. The Holy Spirit makes us true children of God the Father. If we do what He tells us to do, we shall become like Jesus, for Jesus shares with us the Spirit who makes us Sons of God. With the Holy Spirit, we become the true brothers of Jesus. With His help we do what pleases God and Jesus. With His help we do what pleases our parents and teachers. Without the Holy Spirit to give us strength and good ideas, we would find it very difficult to do the works of Jesus. The Holy Spirit helps us to do those works, even if they are difficult, and makes us feel happy when we do them. The Holy Spirit reminds us constantly of the words of Jesus: Love one another as I love you. Share with one another your toys, your joy, your candy, your time. Always, always look out for ways to make people happy. Be always willing to help people.

The presence and dynamic action of the Holy Spirit should be related to the life of the little child. This can be done when something happens in the home. For instance, a child surprises his parent by being helpful on his own, without being asked. A parent can say to the child: "I know who helps you do that. I know who gives you this good idea. It is the Holy Spirit." Or else during evening prayer, parents can recall with children the pleasant moments of the day and thank the Holy Spirit for His help at those particular moments.

Actually, Christians should mention the Holy Spirit and pray to Him more frequently than they do; such awareness is, indeed, a sign of mature Christianity. Thus, the impact of Pentecost should carry forward to the days and months which follow, making all members of the family attentive to the dynamic presence and actual help of the Holy Spirit.

Chapter 11

Mary and the Saints

AFTER Pentecost, the liturgical year calls for the celebration of the mystery of the Church, a mystery with which Mary is so closely connected. Everything which can be said of the mystery of the Church can be said of the mystery of Mary. By relating the two, parents do not run the risk of isolating Marian devotion from the rest of the mystery of salvation. In deeply imbedding Marian devotion within the devotion and liturgy of the Church, parents follow the example set by Vatican II. It is noteworthy that the Council did not issue separate instructions on Mary but inserted a chapter on Mary in the *Constitution on the Church.*

Enter the month of May. Mary's month. Just as Mary is the mother of the Church so is the Church our mother. Just as Mary engenders the life of God in mankind the Church engenders the life of God in mankind through the sacraments. Therefore, every home should have a picture of Mary, the mother of God and the mother of the Church.

Of the various pictures of Mary, I prefer for May a picture in which Mary shows forth her Son. In such pictures, the mother of God presents Jesus who has an expression in which both His humanity and divinity can be read. Other suitable pictures show Mary gathering under her arms or cloak the bishops and priests of the Church. What should be avoided is a picture of Mary totally isolated from Christ and from the Church.

Mary's picture should be placed in the family prayer corner during the month of May and the children should be encouraged to decorate the corner with flowers and candles. In the evening, the family can pray before this picture. Include three Hail Mary's, said with the little children, and end with a Marian hymn.

For little children, an important milestone in the liturgical year comes after the summer months. In the beginning of November, the liturgy is oriented to the mystery of the second coming of the Lord. The mystery must be present in our lives, for the ultimate goal in all Christian life is to join with all the Saints in Heaven. Parents should take advantage of the feast of All Saints to give children a first hint of the joy of heaven.

As a visual aid, parents can write the name of God on a large, brightly-colored poster and have the children decorate portions of the posters. They can do this with crayons or paint or by pasting on decorations. Then parents can write out the names of each child's patron saint for a procession on the evening of All Saints day. Each child can tack the name of his patron on the poster close to the name of God. This symbolizes for the child the closeness of the saint to God and the closeness of the children to God via the patron saint's presence.

On that same evening, parents can use the occasion to tell children something of the lives of their patron saints. A child rejoices in knowing more about the saint whose name he bears. For a child's sense of self, his own name is his primary identification and the Saint becomes someone who is like him. This is due to a child's strong egocentrism. To understand the world around him, he will always begin with his own experience.

A prayer following this story-telling of saints' lives could be a Litany of the Saints with petitions adapted to the particular characteristic for which the saint is honored. This could be followed by a plea to the Saint: "pray for us."

Hail Mary,...Full of Grace...the Lord is with you...

On November 2, when Christians celebrate the feast of those who have died, the family prayer can be centered upon those family members who have departed. Pictures of them can be placed in the prayer corner, for children need to know and want to know about deceased grandparents and other members of the family. The main characteristics of their lives—their virtues, their work, their words can be told. It is important to keep alive the memory of those family members who have died.

Celebration of the Feasts of All Saints and All Souls is bound to elicit questions from little children about souls, heaven, hell and our risen body. Questions of death will be discussed in the next chapter. To help parents in formulating their answers, terms need to be placed in context.

The body must be seen as an expression of the person. It is a sign and an instrument through which we enter into relationship with others and with the world. But its possibilities for communication are limited because it is limited in time and space and because it does not fully reveal the person. The body very often isolates us more than it communicates our deep self. Man's risen body will be the sign and instrument through which persons can express themselves fully and enter into full communion with one another. This mutual transparency and loving relationship with God and with man will be "eternal happiness" and heaven.

Heaven and eternal life should be presented as loving relationships, as being transparent to one another . . . as being fully alive . . . fully aware . . . fully in love with God and with one another . . . a plentitude of life which will never end. This is God's dream which he has made real by sending us Jesus Christ, the first man born to this eternal life. Through Him we have the faith and the hope to share in this new birth to a new world, to a new life. Hell is the exact opposite of heaven, for man through his free choice cuts himself off from God and from those whom God calls to an everlasting joy and life of communion. It is not God who wants hell for man. It is man who refuses to establish loving relationships with God and with people.

The family can pray before a picture of a saint...

Another important point to present to children is that
the kingdom of heaven has *already* started here on earth in
the loving relationships people have with one another and
with God. The same is true of hell. Hell is already here on
earth where people hate their neighbor and hate God.

Therein lies the importance of our options in this life.
God is love and He offers to respond, to answer man's love
freely. Man is free to answer this love by opening himself to
the love of God and neighbor. Man has two choices: to be
with God or else to be without God. Heaven is the fullness
of God within man. Hell is the total absence of God and
love, a total hostility toward neighbor, a total solitude, a
total emptiness.

With this in mind, this chapter can close by suggesting
answers to two questions repeatedly asked by children in
this regard.

CAN I SEE AND FEEL MY SOUL?

No, you cannot see your soul, but in a certain way you
can feel it. For instance, when deep down in yourself, you
feel very, very happy then you can say: "My soul is full of
joy!" You could also say: "My heart is full of joy." Or "I am
full of joy." You might, for instance, say: "My soul is longing
for the Lord!" Or else you could say: "My heart is longing
for the Lord." What makes you a real "I," what makes you
a living and loving person is your body and soul together.
When you feel these things, you feel your soul.

HOW WILL WE BE WHEN WE ARE IN HEAVEN?

We will be like the Lord Jesus and like his mother Mary.
We will be in heaven with our risen body and soul. We don't
know any more than this, except that Jesus tells us we shall
be very happy with God, with Jesus, with the Holy Spirit,
with Mary, with all the saints. We, too, will be saints and so
will all those who love us. Heaven will be a great feast
which will never end.

Chapter 12

Little Children and Death

AT first, for a little child life always overcomes death. Death is a distant fact which does not involve him; he is not personally concerned. Some event external to the child carries the fact of death: an adult conversation that is overheard, a program on television. Death is a plaything: children play dead, "Pow, pow, you're dead;" a child falls down, and then quickly gets up again. A child at play can be killed many times in an afternoon and always return to life.

A child feels himself immortal. He experiences immortality before he realizes that he is mortal. During this first stage, life simply ignores the existence of death as far as the child is concerned. He experiences himself and people who surround him as immortal and not concerned by death.

Death does not threaten his own security in life. Thus he faces death with serenity. When he hears adult conversations about people who died, he does not feel affected as long as the death does not touch his own small secure world.

In the second stage, a child experiences death as a subjective, personal and painful experience with all its emotional and traumatic reverberations. The reaction differs, depending on his relation to the dead one.

For a child, the death of a pet affects him on a deep level; through such an experience a child of three or four discovers for himself the universal law of death. The death of a grandparent whom he sees regularly has far greater impact than the death of a grandparent who lives far away and is seldom seen. The death of a brother or sister or close friend can be shattering, that of a mother or father overwhelming.

In the face of such experiences, a child feels that his own life is threatened. He might revolt against the fact and refuse to accept the possibility of death for those he needs most. He turns to the adults around him and asks: "Do I have to die? Is mommy going to die? Is daddy going to die?"

I remember vividly how the fact of death suddenly struck a four-year-old niece. She was crying in her room when her mother came in and asked what was the matter. "Mommy," she said, "is it true that everybody has to die? Do I have to die?" When her mother said yes, she again burst into tears and said, "I don't want to die. I don't want to go to heaven. I don't want you to leave me. I don't want daddy to die." Her parents had no idea where and how she came to realize that she herself would die someday, but the fact was there. From that day forward, she was very much concerned about death.

As strange as it may sound to adult ears, children can also apply the Christian message to the fact of death and stress the joy of going to heaven. A four-year-old nephew once rushed to his grandmother shortly after the death of his grandfather and said: "Oh, how good! Pop-pop is in heaven. Is it true? Is it really true? What about us then? Why can't we go to heaven?" A niece said, "Grandmother, Pop-pop is in heaven. Are you happy now? He's with God. He's no longer sick. He no longer hurts."

But this same grandchild soon came to realize that death means separation. A few weeks later on a visit to her grandmother, she complained, "But grandma, I think it's enough now. Pop-pop should come back to us from heaven. I don't think God should keep him so long. I want Pop-pop to be with us. Why doesn't God let him come back? God is not nice to keep him in heaven."

For a little child, awareness of the separation caused by

A child's first experience with death often involves his dog...

death creates pain. Death means the loss of someone who provides security and love. Reactions vary. Some children seem resigned, others cry silently, some become desperate and refuse any food. Many children become pale, experience nightmares. Others might even appear as if they couldn't care less, adopting a defensive attitude.

The adult response requires tact, tenderness, compassion and the full force of love. The child needs a reassuring smile, a kiss, the comfort of two arms holding him tightly. Some children will rebel before the mystery of death, especially if someone they need has been taken away. They will accuse God of being bad for taking a loved one away from them.

Teacher or parent should accept these accusations without feeling obliged to answer them. Once again, a smile, a gesture may be what is needed right then. Only later, when the shock has passed, can a parent tell his child that through death God gives the person who died a new life. Death is, as one of my nieces put it, "a little like baptism."

Through death, God gives the deceased a life that shall never end and that we shall enjoy, too, for some day children will join their parents and grandparents. Together, they will be happy forever.

Very gradually, a child will understand that there is no true separation between the living and the dead. Through memory, through love, through affection, all can remain together, and all are together as a matter of fact. Awareness of such togetherness is reached by the child through the attitude of the adults surrounding him. They give witness to the children of their Christian hope and faith.

There is no reason to be evasive or to dismiss a child's concern about death. It won't work. And it is not the Christian's way. The moment of Jesus' own death need only be recalled to make the point that death must be confronted honestly—in its pain and in its significance. Expressing the total solitude of that moment, Jesus said: "Father, why have you forsaken me?" Jesus never showed a shallow optimism when facing the anxiety of human death, but he also placed total trust in God his Father. At the moment of death, his ultimate act of faith was trust in eternal life.

Accepting the unknown is not easy for man; it is not easy even for a Christian. It certainly is more difficult for a child whose focus is here-and-now. In many ways, the dramatic experience of death can be compared with the experience of birth, the difference being that man isn't conscious at the moment of birth. At the moment of death, man can be conscious of this new birth, this new jump into the unknown.

Here parents face children's questions about *what* and *how: What* does heaven look like? *What* will we look like? *How* will it be in heaven, in hell? *How* will we get there?

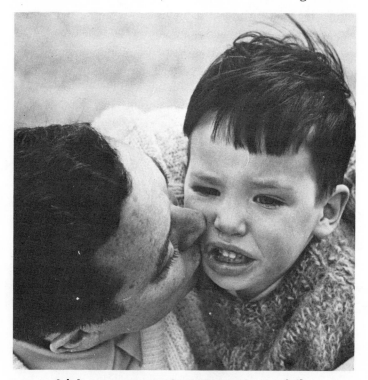

**Adult response requires compassion and the
full force of love . . .**

What shall we eat? I have tried to answer specific questions in a special section at the end of the book, but it is important here to stress that adults should be ready to admit that they don't know all the answers. Parents can say to children: "I don't know *how*. I don't know *what* it looks like. That's something with which God wants to surprise us. But it certainly will be beautiful, more wonderful than anything we can imagine."

What is important is that adults bear witness to the child by strong faith and belief in what Jesus tells Christians through the Gospel about death and eternal life. Adults have the duty of proclaiming through their attitude and their words the message of Christian hope when death strikes their family.

The Apocalypse tells Christians that heaven will be a state of life where there will be no tears, no more suffering, no more separation. We will be together with God and with all those whom we love. We will live in peace, in love, in joy, in thanksgiving and praise—forever.

Christian hope is the certainty of being together in peace and joy and of sharing life and love in heaven. This should be the normal Christian attitude and it is important that children sense this spiritual attitude of expectation, of desire for heaven, for communion with man and God.

Parents can say to children: "When a person dies, he receives the joy of heaven. He is with God, with Jesus, with the angels and with the saints. He joins those who have already gone to heaven, those he loved."

In speaking of those who have already died, parents can evoke their memory, point out their nearness to God in the joy and glory of heaven and remind children that the departed can care for us even more than if they were still on earth. The presence of the departed can be evoked by a picture with flowers in front of it, by a prayer to God on behalf of them, by a few words addressed to the deceased in a prayer. Of course, this should not be morbidly exaggerated.

Remarks made in the course of family life can also help to make children sense the continued presence of the departed. A mother can congratulate her child for a good deed by adding that a deceased grandparent is proud of him. Or at a time when a family is considering a decision, one parent might say, "Let's see. What would grandfather have done in this situation?"

It can't be said too often. Children discover and experience the mystery of death through the attitudes of adults. Their reactions will be patterned on adult reactions. It is less important, therefore, to explain to children the mystery of death than to have them share in an atmosphere of Christian peace and hope. Children can only experience this through the attitudes and behavior of adults. Of course, it is not easy to express these Christian attitudes of Chrisian hope and belief in the face of the death of a loved one, but one must pray for such strength.

Unfortunately, day in, day out, many adults do as children do: they refuse to face the fact of death, they ignore it. Instead, a child should be initiated into the Christian meaning of death before he is faced with it abruptly as a sudden and brutal fact. Parents and other adults must approach the subject with care, tact and prudence, but approach it they must. The sensitivity, the development and the experiences of the particular child must be taken into account. There is no simple formula except that of paying attention to the specific child.

In this matter as in all religious education for little children, parents and grandparents play the paramount role. Teachers are very secondary and very limited in what they can do to help the child face this mystery. Happy then are those children whose parents and grandparents help them face death, even their own personal death, with Christian hope and faith in the light of the resurrection.

Chapter 13

The Special
Role of Grandparents

GRANDPARENTS fill a special role in the religious education and formation of children, a role woven into their special position in family life. Through grandparents, a family senses its history and unity; through them, wisdom and experience are shared; through them, a sense of continuity and of achievement is passed on. The presence of grandparents gives children a feeling of roots, a sense of belonging.

The importance of grandparents in the life of little children is immeasurable. A young child with the good fortune to have a grandparent nearby benefits in countless ways. He has a place to share his joys and his sorrows; a place to find a sympathetic and patient listener; a place to be loved.

Grandparents have the time to marvel with grandchildren over their discoveries of the world. They can be on hand to congratulate a child on the house of blocks he has built, or the picture he has colored. Young children want to be recognized by adults. Grandparents provide such recognition in heartwarming abundance. Often mothers are too busy and fathers are away at work, preventing a child from sharing their enthusiasm. Grandparents have the great opportunity to be present.

For little children, grandparents stand out as adults who devote time to them, who can be counted on, who love them.

A grandparent's home can be a haven, a place where security, attention and love await the child. Grandparents, in turn, have the precious luxury of time to devote to little children. While mothers who stay at home have great demands put on their time, the increasing number of working mothers find it even more important to rely on grandparents. To go to grandfather's house becomes a treat, a joy for little children, while it is often a necessity when parents have to work, handle other duties or face crises of one kind or another.

Grandparents, then, can play an important part in shaping the personality of a child, thereby gaining the satisfaction of filling a vital role. Whether the contact between grandparent and child is sporadic or constant, something vital is going on—for both of them.

A child without grandparents can feel a lack of roots. He misses a chance to link up with the past. When given such a chance, children embrace it eagerly. This is evident in the way they rush to look at family photograph albums, asking questions, listening to stories, getting explanations of what the family was doing, wearing, where it was going, what was happening. Questions and answers about the "old-

Presence of grandparents gives a feeling of roots...

en days" locate a child historically in his own small world
and provide him with a sense of security and a feeling of
belonging.

Of course, there is no denying the danger of selfishness
in grandparent-grandchild relations. Sometimes, grandparents try to buy the affection of little ones by spoiling them,
by constantly buying them gifts, by giving them money
when they visit. This distorts the relationship and upsets
many a parent during such visits. Grandparents need to be
reminded that grandchildren respond most to those who do
not abandon their position as self-confident adults, who know
where to draw the line, who do not abandon all discipline
and become completely indulgent.

Children immediately feel the difference between a
grandparent who is self-centered and a grandparent whose
interest is in the growth and development of the child. Children bask in the helpful sunshine of grandparents who teach
them how to cook, how to knit, how to play cards, how to
build a fire, how to use a hammer, how to rake leaves, how
to wash a car. Children can learn so many things in their
grandparents' home by watching and imitating.

Clearly, the isolation of older people in Florida or Cali-
fornia enclaves—no matter how comfortable—is misguided. It
ignores the vital need of the younger generation for grandparents who have wisdom and time to offer them. It deprives children of the perspective that older people have
acquired and it deprives older people of a satisfying role in
family life.

In terms of religious formation, grandparents can often
see more readily what is essential and what is not. Grandparents develop a philosophy of life based on long experience. Their location at a certain distance from the hurly-
burly of the working world can give them a new vision of
people and events approached through their grandchildren,
an approach so highly praised by Christ in the Gospel. In
Matthew (18:3-5), Jesus said of the child He put in the midst
of the disciples: "Truly I say to you, unless you turn and become like little children, you will never enter into the king-

dom of heaven. Whoever humbles himself like a little child, he is the greatest in the kingdom of heaven. Whoever receives one such child in my name, receives me."

This gospel quotation concerning the spirit of childhood can be specifically applied to grandparents who consciously or unconsciously follow Christ's command. They have the rare capacity of wondering and marveling at all that surrounds them. They seem to experience in a new way and in a new depth. And they do this in collaboration with their grandchildren. Grandparents more than parents experience the days as gifts presented to them by God to bring their life to fullness. This is why their inner, spiritual life can grow to a greater and greater attachment to true values and a deeper vision of life which prepares their vision of eternal life, beauty, and love. Every day is a new day for them to celebrate God's creativity and love. Small children intuitively sense in grandparents the spiritual values and attitudes which express themselves by inner peace and attachment to

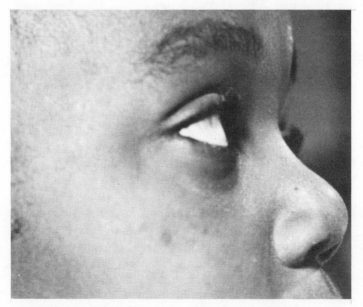

Grandparents help answer the why's and how's...

real values. Grandparents and grandchildren somehow share a similar capacity to celebrate life.

Fortunate are those children whose grandmother takes them to city parks to marvel with them at the beauty of the tree in blossom or the lake reflecting the sunlight. Fortunate is the child who has walked through woods and fields with a grandfather for whom nature is the sign and symbol of God, creator of heaven and earth. Fortunate are those grandparents who become more and more sensitive to the beauty of the world. Fortunate is the child who can turn to a grandparent with questions as he discovers new aspects of life around him. Fortunate is the child who at his grandmother's table has experienced thanksgiving prayer. Fortunate is the child who has experienced the deep joy and loving presence of a grandparent and from this experience learned those moments of silence and intimacy which lead to contemplation and prayer.

Grandparents share with parents the great responsibility for answering little children's questions. Answers—coming from adults trusted and loved by children—carry much weight. Answers to questions with the endless *why's, how's* and *what's* influence a child's religious development and shape his entire view of life. Grandparents as well as parents must answer with care and seriousness. Children deserve more than flippant or offhanded answers. They need much more, and so adults must be deeply concerned and attentive in answering questions, especially religious ones. Rather than improvise with uncertainty, it is better to say: "I don't know right now. Let me think about it. Maybe I'll be able to tell you tomorrow."

Aunts and uncles, especially if they are unmarried and live close to the family, also have the opportunity to answer children's questions and to listen to what either delights or disturbs them. Aunts and uncles should make themselves available to nephews and nieces, for children will often come to them when they are in trouble with their own parents. There are some questions they wouldn't ask their parents, but which they would ask uncles and aunts. Children tend especially to ask them questions about the beginning of life.

Grandparents are often asked about the end of life. Here, adults may miss the opportunity of having children grow in a Christian vision of man and of the world. They often are so embarrassed by children's questions on death, they don't answer or they evade the question. What a pity, for isn't death the real goal and aim of this life? Isn't this life given to us to shape our own death and eternal future? Fortunate are those children who feel free to ask their grandparents and parents about the beginning of life and the beginning of that new life which comes after death. Fortunate are those children who receive from grandparents answers expressing Christian hope in the resurrection of the whole person and in the coming of a new world—heaven.

Often, grandchildren ask grandparents metaphysical questions, which are a real challenge to their understanding of faith in God. This is fitting, for the growth in faith has no end in man's lifetime. Old age brings both the opportunity and the impetus to purify faith and to meditate upon the ultimate goal of life. It is man left alone with his ultimate choice—in favor of God or against God. The loving grandparent who bears witness to his Christian faith and choice bestows a powerful religious lesson and bequeaths a priceless gift to a grandchild.

Chapter 14

The Most Important Classroom

*T*ODAY'S religious leaders—bishops, pastors and religious teachers—stress the aim of religious education as nurturing the faith of a child so that it can grow. Religious education, therefore, is more than indoctrination. It is a matter of living faith, a matter of Christian values and of a Christian world vision.

At no age is this growth process more important and more delicate to achieve than on the pre-school level. Psychologists emphasize the importance of these tender years in shaping the personality of a person.

What is true in personality development is also true in shaping Christian faith. The responsibility for this growth in faith in a young child rests primarily with Christian parents, their children's first catechists. When parents ask the Church to accept their child in the community of believers, through Baptism—a sacrament of faith—the child receives the faith of his parent which in turn is rooted in the faith of the Christian community. The faith of the infant is a seed to be nurtured in its first and natural environment—the family.

Christian parents, therefore, have a direct responsibility for the religious formation and growth of faith in their children. They are the first teachers; the home is the first classroom.

In official Church documents, the parent's role is fre-

The most important school of religion...

quently emphasized when giving directives to those responsible for Christian education of children. Parents are always
mentioned immediately after the bishop; they come before
pastors, other teachers and the catechists in the community.
Parents exercise their lay apostolate in the Church by living
and by revealing the Christian mystery in their family. Their
Christian responsibility as Christians in the world is fulfilled
primarily with their children. No one can fully substitute for
them.

Through the sacrament of marriage, parents have received a grace and a mission to create a Christian family
that shall become a living cell of the Church. How can parents achieve this educational mission in the Church? Too
often in past centuries, mainly after the counter-Reforma-
tion, Christians have tended to think that the communication
of faith had to be achieved in terms of doctrine that should
be explained and then memorized. The emphasis in religious
education was put on creating agencies for communicating
doctrine. The very names of agencies like the Confraternity
of Christian Doctrine reflect this emphasis.

Today, research in the fields of cultural anthropology
and sociology, as well as psychology, provides clear evidence
that the process of growth in the faith does not lie only
within the intellect. It is closely related with belonging to a
group. Religious psychology shows that religion is located in
a person's deep emotions and that it is the result of the way
in which he was socialized by the adults who cared for him
as a child.

Dr. Ellis Nelson, head of the department of religious
education at Union Theological Seminary, makes this important observation: "Faith is communicated to the person
by a community of believers, and a meaning of faith is developed by its members out of their history, by their interaction with each other and in relation to the events that
take place in their lives."

Thus, religious education is lifelong, a continuing process which takes place in a community of believers. It cannot be encompassed in a doctrinal course. Scholars in the

field of cultural anthropology and sociology have shown that the basic unit of reality in the process is the group to which the person belongs.

The natural agency for communicating the faith is the community of believers, and for the young child *this first community is his family*. The child absorbs the culture and the faith of the family; he shares in his family's world vision and values. The role, then, of the family in socializing the child and communicating the faith is fundamental.

However, in emphasizing the role of parents, many religious educators have assumed that parents have the skills needed to teach the faith in the home. My own evidence and that of my colleagues show that most parents say they are willing—but not able. They are eager to meet their responsibilities but feel at a loss in matters of religious teaching for pre-school children.

It is clear that more attention must be paid to the continuous training of parents so they can grow in their own Christian faith, values and knowledge. Only on this basis will they be able to achieve their role of Christian parents within the home. But it is not necessary for parents to become skilled teachers. They are called upon to be Christian witnesses.

It is in the family atmosphere that Christian life is transmitted to the child. What matters is what a mother or father says and does, whether at the table, in front of the television set, in the neighborhood, or at the store. Through their life together with the children, parents share themselves, their values, their way of approaching the world and their faith.

In short, a Christian family's way of life should naturally relate daily events to the Gospel brought to us by Jesus Christ. The family's main contribution will be that of communicating the Christian world view and values. This will be achieved informally much more often than formally, in living out actions and reactions that reveal the Christian dimension and values for whatever happens.

Christian parents must help children discover and see in secular experiences the Christian dimension and meaning.

Parents of pre-schoolers are often concerned about what they can do that is specifically religious. They ask: What shall we say about God? Which prayer shall we teach? Which visual aid is best?

All these are important and this book tries to help parents answer these questions. But the essential contribution of parents lies less in what parents say than in what they are, and in what they think, and how they live. It lies in their Christian witness—their attitudes and behavior, the love, courage and trust in God that they express in the home and in responding to world events, their respect at home and in church when they pray with their family, their capacity for wonder, praise and thanksgiving. All this deeply impregnates the young child and shapes his faith.

This Christian witness is the most important contribution of parents to the religious education of their children.

In the increasingly secular world into which parents send their children, it is certain that the family will have even a more important contribution to make in matters of Christian education and formation. In order to strengthen this contribution, families and parents stand in greater need of help. This help must come from the local community of believers primarily in the form of ongoing theological education for parents.

The local Christian community must help parents fulfill their responsibilities. This is true on the pre-school level and it is also true when parents send their children to Sunday School, CCD or parish schools. The school must keep in close contact with parents, exchange information, and facilitate collaboration between home and school. But in the first place, nothing can substitute for religious experience and witness that children encounter in their family situation.

For the pre-school child, the die is cast with parents, his first catechists, and the home—his first and most important religious classroom.

Appendix I

A CHRISTMAS EVE CELEBRATION
IN THE HOME

Materials Needed

Place a manger on a small table in the living room, close to the Christmas tree.

Place some kind of sand box in front of and below the manger, so that the tops of the candles, once they are stuck into the sand, are even with the base or floor of the manger. Candlestick holders can be used.

A candle for each participant.

The figures by the manger include Mary and Joseph, animals.

The Bible (or Missal) should be off center and in a place of honor (on a stand, desk, table, etc.). The texts for the readings (found on these pages) should be inserted into the Bible or Missal.

Different Roles for the Celebration

Leader: father or mother, or older sister or brother
Reader(s): father or mother, or older sister or brother
All the children and other members of the household.

1. CANDLE PROCESSION TOWARD THE MANGER

Everyone should assemble in the living room or in an adjoining room. The youngest child carries the Infant Jesus. All the other members of the family carry their lighted candles, which they place in the sand box in front of the manger.

Preparation:

Leader: For many weeks we have been preparing our selves to celebrate the feast of Christmas. Now, with everyone in the whole world, we are going to celebrate the birthday of Jesus. Today we have prepared a manger. Mary and Joseph are already by the manger. They are waiting for us because we are going to place the Infant Jesus in the manger. Now we are all going to the manger. (Name) will go in first, and he will place the Infant Jesus in the manger. Then we will all bring our joy and our light to the manger. We will put our candles in the sand box in front of the manger. (At this time the leader lights his candle, then those of the small children and the other members of the family.)

Light

Leader: Look how beautiful our candles are. There is a beautiful light which shines and fills us with light and joy. In order to show our Lord all our joy on this Christmas Eve, we are going to bring our light to the manger. So that He can see the joy which is in our hearts; while we proceed to the manger, we will sing "Rejoice, rejoice, O Israel; To you shall come Emmanuel" (or the entire song, "O Come, Emmanuel;" or something similar).

Procession to the Manger

(The song is directed by the leader, or a record can be played as an accompaniment to the singers.)

2. AT THE CRIB (All remain standing)

Leader: Now that we are all gathered around the manger, we can place our candles in the box in front of the manger. (When this is done) Listen to the Word of God.

First Reading

Reader: (stands in front of the entire family and faces them with the Bible or Missal open, and reads the adapted text

given here.) Listen to the Word of God.
"God loves us very much. God loves us so much
that he gives us His Son Jesus."

Gesture of Adoration

Leader: Let us kneel down to adore the Lord Jesus. (The
leader then leads in the singing of these verses from "O
Come, Ye Faithful":)
"O, Come let us adore Him, O, Come let us adore
Him. O, Come let us adore Him, Christ the Lord."

Second Reading

Leader: Let us all sit down, around the manger, so we can
all listen to the beautiful story of Christmas which is written in the Bible.

Reader: (waits for everyone to be seated before beginning
the reading. He reads distinctly and slowly.)

"On the first Christmas night the shepherds were
watching over their sheep in the countryside near
Bethlehem. All of a sudden, the glory of God surrounded them with its light, and an angel of the
Lord said to them:

I bring good news to you, which will be a great joy
for all people. Today, in the town of Bethlehem,
A Saviour is born to you. You will find him wrapped
in strips of cloth, and lying in a manger.

And then, all the angels began to praise God, singing:

Glory to God in the highest, and on earth peace to
men of good will."   (Luke 2:8-14 adapted)

Leader: We could join the angels by singing with them
while clapping our hands:
"Glory to God, Glory. O Praise Him, Alleluia.

Glory to God, Glory. O Praise the name of the Lord."

Family Conversation

The father or mother could question the children concerning this first part of the text. These questions help the children to reconstruct the text and the message given to the shepherds by the angel, that is: God the Father sends his son Jesus to be our Savior.

Some suggested questions: Who was in the countryside that night? What happened? What did the angel say? What else did he say? What did the angels sing?

Leader: Let us sing a song that tells us about this silent night.
Suggested songs:

> "Silent Night"
> "O Come All Ye Faithful"
> "Angels We Have Heard on High"

Third Reading

(A different person could be used for each reading)
"Now, when the angels had gone, The Shepherds said to one another:
Let us go to Bethlehem, and see what has happened there.
So they hurried away, and they found Mary and Joseph, and the Baby lying in a manger. They looked at the child, and told Mary and Joseph what the angel had told them. Mary listened and watched. She kept in her heart everything she saw and heard. And all who heard these things were surprised and very happy. They all came to adore the Lord Jesus.
After the shepherds went away They told everyone What they had seen And what they had heard. To-

gether with all men of good will, "They sang about the praise and glory of God."

Family Conversation

Again, the father or mother helps the children to reconstruct the text, by asking questions.

Suggested questions: When the shepherds arrived at the manger, what did they see? (They found a baby like all other babies—he sleeps, he cries, he needs his mother—he was born like us.) When they see the baby, they kneel and adore—Why? (This is a very special baby; his birth is announced by the angels; a great light, the glory of God, the joy, the songs, the good news.)

Why is Jesus' birth so special? (Jesus is the Son of God; God has sent his Son to save us, to give us peace. Jesus comes to tell us how much God loves us; he teaches us to love God and to love each other.)

Prayers of Petition

Leader:

Lord Jesus, give us your joy in our hearts. (All repeat) Lord Jesus, give your light to the world. (All repeat) Lord Jesus, give your peace to all nations. (All repeat)

(At this time, individual members of the family could give their own intentions.)

Prayer

Leader:

Holy Father, You have given us Jesus your Son. He comes to save us. He brought us your light and your peace. That is why, with the angels and the people of the whole world, We give you thanks on this Christmas Eve.

Song

Leader: Let us sing our joy and praise to the Lord. Suggested songs:

"Joy to the World"

"Praise to the Lord"

(Records of Christmas songs could also be played.)

End

Leader: Tonight, we know a little better how much God loves us. He is the one who gives us our most beautiful gift. To show the Lord how much we love one another, we will now bring the gifts which we have prepared, and put them under the tree. Tomorrow we will give these gifts to one another, because we want to show and tell those who love us, how much we love them with all our hearts.

(This last part involving gifts could be modified to fit the family custom.)

Christmas music could be played while the children prepare for bed.

Appendix II

THE 76 MOST ASKED QUESTIONS
AND THEIR ANSWERS

Whether or not children live in Christian families, they ask
religious questions. The best rule to follow is to answer
truthfully and simply. But many parents are embarrassed or
confused when little children ask about God, death, heaven,
hell. Such questions can embarrass parents when they are
forced to confront their own commitments; or parents are
confused when they are forced to confront their own limited knowledge of the subject matter. Because children both
need and deserve meaningful answers and because parents
both need and deserve help in giving these answers, the following answers are provided for questions commonly asked
by little children.

The suggested answers are meant as background and
orientation. Therefore, they tend to be long. Out of them,
however, each parent can fashion his own answer *in the language and at the level of his or her child*. Most important,
dialogue must be established between parent and child.
These answers will help to establish that dialogue.

WHO IS GOD?

God is someone who knows you by your name, because
He loves you. You are very special to Him. God is someone
who knows each one of us by our name because He loves us

all. Your father and mother know you by your name because they love you more than anyone on earth. God loves you even more than your mother and daddy. We, too, know God by His name. God is pleased when we call Him by His name, when we speak to Him. God has many names. His most beautiful name is *God our Father*.

WHY DO WE CALL GOD OUR FATHER?

We call God Our Father, because God loves us. We are His children—He is our Heavenly Father. Once, when Jesus was praying, one of His friends asked Him: "Lord, teach us how to speak to God. Lord, teach us how to pray." Jesus answered: "When you pray say: Our Father . . . hallowed be thy name . . ."

CAN I SEE GOD?

No, not yet. God is so different from us that we can't see Him with our eyes. Some day, in heaven, we will see Him face to face. But we already can see something of the great beauty and love of God. When we look at the sun, the moon and the stars; when we look at the ocean, the rivers and the mountains; when we look at the trees, the plants and the animals; when we look at all the things God has made and given to us, we can see something of the great beauty and power of God. When we look at our father and our mother who love one another and their children, they show us something of the love which God has for every one of us. Then we see something of the way God loves and takes care of His children.

WHERE IS GOD?

God is everywhere. God is in heaven and God is on earth. God is in every place where there is life. God is in every place where there is joy. God is in every place where there is beauty. God is in every place where there is love. God is in every place where people love one another. God is wherever people live in peace with one another.

WHAT DOES GOD LOOK LIKE?

I don't know, because God is so different from us. I cannot see Him with my eyes. I cannot hear Him with my ears. All I know is that He is greater and more powerful than anything we can see or think of. What I know is that He takes care and loves us more than anyone we can think of.

WHAT DOES GOD DO?

God gives life to everything. God gives life and love to everyone. It is God who gives life to all that is alive. It is God who gives love to all who love one another. It is God who has made heaven and earth and all that is alive. It is God who keeps everything alive.

CAN GOD SEE ME?

Yes, God sees you always, because God loves you. But God does not need eyes, like yours. Your eyes only help you to see some things. With your eyes, you cannot see people when they are far away. You cannot see Daddy when he is at work. God sees everything and everyone, because He knows and loves us even more than a mother loves her children. He knows everything we think of; He knows the people we long for. Yes, God even knows the secrets we keep in our heart.

DOES GOD KNOW EVERYTHING?

Yes, God knows everything because He gives life to all that is alive. Yes, God knows everyone because He gives us life and loves us. When you love someone very, very much, you know a lot about him. Your mother loves you very much; that's why she knows when your heart is sad or when you are afraid. Your father and mother know so much about you, even some of the things you keep secret in your heart, because they love you. God loves you even more than your father and mother. That's why He knows you so well. That's why He wants always to be with you. He knows when you get up in the morning. He knows when you go to bed at night. He knows the secrets you keep in your heart. He knows when you are happy and when you are sad. Night and day, God is with you, because He loves you.

CAN GOD HEAR ME?

Yes, God can hear you, but He needs no ear to hear you because God is so different from us. When you speak to God He hears your prayer. When you sing to God, He hears your song. When you whisper He hears you. When you make a drawing for God, He knows what you want to tell Him with your drawing. Sometimes, you might think that you are left alone in your room. Sometimes, you might be a little frightened. Well, you should not be. You are never alone. God is always with you, because He loves you. He takes care of you. You cannot see Him with your eyes, but He sees you. You cannot hear Him with your ears, but He hears you.

CAN I SPEAK TO GOD?

You can speak always and everywhere to God and He will hear you. You can tell God how happy you are that He is always with you. One of God's friends said this prayer to God: "I love God, because He is always with me. I love God, because He hears me. He listens to me when I speak to Him. God is good and God loves me. He always takes care of me; day and night He watches over me" (Adapted from Psalm 116). Shall we say this prayer to God together?

DOES GOD LIVE IN A HOUSE?
DOES GOD HAVE A YARD?

No, God does not live in a house with a yard like ours. God does not live in a house, on a street with a number and a zip code. God is so different from us that He does not need a house. But God lives in all homes where people love one another. God lives in the hearts of all those who want to be His children. And all those who love God and who are His children like to gather in a special house, a house of prayer which we call the church. We also can call that house the house of God. In our neighborhood we have such a house. Every Sunday God invites all His friends to gather in His house. Every Sunday God invites His friends to a feast. Every Sunday God speaks to us. We listen to His words. Every Sunday we sing our joy to God and speak to Him. Some of the beautiful words we say to God are: "We praise You, we bless You, we adore You, we give You thanks!" When God's children gather in God's house, God is with them in a very special way.

HOW CAN YOU SAY GOD IS GOOD IF HE PUNISHES CHILDREN WHEN THEY ARE BAD?

God never punishes naughty children. Children punish themselves when they are naughty. When children are naughty, they choose to separate themselves from those who love them; they choose to pout and turn away from others. When children are naughty, they choose to turn away from God. When people turn away from those who love them, they hurt themselves. They feel lonesome and sad. God never wants to punish His children, because He loves us always, even when we do wrong. God is always waiting for us to turn back to Him, to our parents, to our brothers and sisters, to our friends. God always wants us to come back to Him and to those who love us. God is always willing to forgive us. When we have done something wrong, God calls us back and helps us not to do wrong again.

WHY DOES GOD ALLOW LIGHTNING?
WHY DOES GOD ALLOW FLOODS?

Everything that God does is good. But things can be dangerous. We need light; light is good. But lightning can be dangerous. We need water; water is good. But water can be dangerous and become a flood. There are still many things that need to be mastered on the earth. God wants us to work with Him to make this earth a more beautiful place to live in. He gives every one of us something of His power and intelligence. God also gives us great responsibilities. God asks us to use these gifts to organize the world better. With the strength and the intelligence we have received from God, we can protect ourselves from the rain and the lightning by building homes. We also build dams to protect ourselves against floods. There are many things we can do to use all the means God has given us to protect ourselves when things become dangerous.

DOES GOD MAKE EVERYTHING?
DOES HE MAKE AIRPLANES AND TUNNELS?

That's a good question. No, God does not make the airplanes and the tunnels. People make all of these things. But God does give people everything they need to make things like bridges and tunnels. The most beautiful thing God has made is people. God has made man very powerful. He has given to man a little of His intelligence. He has given to man a little of His love. With this power and this love people can do many marvelous things. They can go to the moon; they can build houses and throughways, bridges and airplanes. God is very pleased when He sees people using the gifts they have received to make the world a better place in which to live. God wants us to organize the world. He wants us to work with Him. When we see all that men can do we should thank God and say to Him: "How great and powerful You must be, when I see how great and powerful You have made man" (Adapted Ps. 8).

WHY DOES GOD KEEP BAD PEOPLE ALIVE?

God does not want the death of people who are bad. He wants them to become good. God loves them always because they are His children. God always is willing to forgive those who hurt us. God knows what is deep in our hearts. He knows that even in the hearts of bad people there are still goodness and love. Often people become bad because nobody loves them. Even the greatest criminals are still able to love and are willing to help people. God loves them. God wants them to become good. But God does not force them. He waits for those who have done wrong to freely return to Him and to other people who still love them.

I ASKED GOD TO HEAL MY GRANDMOTHER AND HE DID NOT. WHY?

When you pray for someone you love very much, you always should ask God to give to that person what is best for him or her. Maybe the greatest happiness for your grandmother is to die and to go to Heaven and to join those whom she has loved on earth—your grandfather, her own mother and father. Yes, the greatest happiness for people is to be with God and with those whom they love. The greatest happiness is to share God's love and joy and peace forever. If your grandmother is sick, you should pray for her, and ask God for what is best for her. You should be very kind to her; you should give her joy. God will give her strength if she is sick. God knows better than we do what your grandmother needs so she can be really happy. We can put all our trust in God. He knows what grandmother needs.

THOSE WHO DO NOT KNOW GOD, THOSE WHO DO NOT BELIEVE IN GOD, WILL THEY GO TO HEAVEN?

Hundreds and hundreds of people do not know God, it is true. Most often this is not their own fault. Maybe they have never met people who know God. Maybe they have never been told about God. Still, those who do not know God often do all that God asks us to do. God's spirit helps them secretly. We say they follow their conscience. They love one another, they help one another, they forgive, they share. . . . Without knowing, they love God and they love people. They will certainly be with us in heaven. There, they will know God and they will be happy forever. Even here and now we could help some people to know and to love God by loving one another. We can ask God to give those who don't know Him some special light to help them discover God in this life. If they knew about God how much happier they would be!

WHO IS JESUS?

Jesus is the Son of God the Father. God loves us so much that He sent us Jesus. Jesus knows God the Father better than anyone because He is God's own Son. Jesus comes to tell us all about His Father. It is Jesus who teaches us that God is our Father, and that we are His children. It is also Jesus who shows us how to love one another. If we want to know more about Jesus, we can read His words in the Gospel, or better, we can listen to the good news which is read to us in church.

WAS JESUS A BOY LIKE ME?

Yes, just like you, Jesus was born a baby. He grew like all of us. God chose Mary to become the Mother of Jesus and to take care of Jesus. God also asked a man, Joseph, to take care of Jesus and His mother, Mary. Jesus had a home, He had friends. He learned how to walk and how to talk. When Jesus grew up, He went to school to learn how to read and write. He also went to God's House with His parents. Jesus loved to speak to God; He loved to pray. When Jesus spoke to God He would say: "My father . . . "

IS JESUS BORN AGAIN EVERY YEAR AT CHRISTMAS?

No, just like you, Jesus was born only once. This happened many years ago in a city called Bethlehem. Every year at Christmas, we celebrate the birthday of Jesus. When we celebrate your birthday, you do not become a baby or be born all over again, do you? No, not at all. The reason we are so happy to celebrate your birthday is because you are growing. The more you grow, the more important you become to us. The more you grow, the more we need you. For Jesus, it is just the same. Every year at Christmas we celebrate His birthday. Every year we get to know Jesus better. He becomes more and more important for us. Every year we want to thank our Heavenly Father for sending us His Son,

Jesus. Every year we ask Jesus to stay with us and to become more and more alive in us. If we open our hearts to
Jesus, we will be able to love people more and more, to
make peace, to help people, to give thanks to God our Father.

WHERE IS JESUS NOW?

Jesus is everywhere as is God, His Father. Jesus is with
His Father in heaven and He is with us on earth. Jesus is
everywhere people love one another. Jesus is risen. He is
alive. He lives in us. Just like God the Father, Jesus knows
me by my name. Just like God the Father, Jesus sees me and
hears me.

WHY DID JESUS HAVE TO DIE?

Because Jesus wanted to live and die just like us. Because He wants to share with us His new life. Just like Jesus,
God our Father will give us a new life after we die. Just like
Jesus, if we put all our trust in God, He will give us a new
life, a life of happiness, joy and peace which shall never
end.

WHY DID PEOPLE KILL JESUS?

That's a long story which I will make short. Jesus, when
He was thirty years old, when He was a man, left His home
and His parents. Jesus started going from one city to another. He was teaching people and telling them about God,
His Father. He told people how much God loves us and how
we can love God in return. He showed people how to love
God the Father. He would often speak to His Father. He
also showed people how to love one another. He would say,
love one another, even your enemy; forgive always and always, make peace, share, always say the truth. . . . Some people were disturbed by the words of Jesus because He asked
them to do things they thought were too difficult for them
to do. They wanted Jesus to stop speaking. The best way to
stop Jesus was to kill Him. They came to Jesus and asked

Him: "Who are you? Are you the Son of God?" Jesus answered: "Yes, I am." They said: "You are guilty and must be put to death because you say that you are the Son of God." That's why they killed Jesus. Jesus freely gave His life for us, and even for those who killed Him, because He loves us all and wants us to share in His everlasting happiness. There is no greater love than to give your life for somebody else. That is what Jesus did for all of us. He shares with us a new life, His life, so that we shall never die.

WHY DO WE ALWAYS SEE JESUS ON A CROSS?

We often see pictures with Jesus on a cross because we who are Jesus' friends want to remember that Jesus gave His life for us on a cross. Many years ago, people would use a cross to kill people. Today we use weapons. But we have also other pictures of Jesus. Some pictures show us Jesus teaching. Other pictures show us Jesus Who is risen and is in the glory of God. Jesus did not remain dead. He rose from the dead. Jesus is more powerful than death. Today Jesus is alive; today Jesus can be with us always and everywhere.

I WOULD LIKE TO SEE JESUS

You cannot see Jesus with your eyes. Just like you can't see God His Father. Now that Jesus is risen, He has a new body which we cannot see with our eyes. One day, however, we shall see Him and we also shall see God, His Father. Today you already see something of Jesus when you see Jesus' friends gathered in God's house, singing the glory of God. When the priest speaks to us, he speaks in the name of Jesus. When the priest forgives us, he forgives in the name of Jesus. When we see people who love one another and help one another, we see something of Jesus.

WILL JESUS COME DOWN ON EARTH AGAIN?

Jesus is already on earth and in heaven, but one day we shall see Him face to face. That shall be on the last day, when Jesus will come back and show Himself to us with His risen body.

WHO IS THE HOLY SPIRIT?

The Holy Spirit is a person Who is always with us. We call Him the Spirit of God. Just like God the Father, we can't see the Holy Spirit with our eyes. We receive the Holy Spirit the day we are baptized. He is at work in our heart. He makes us children of God. It is the Holy Spirit Who helps us to love God and people with all our heart. It is the Holy Spirit Who gives us good ideas to make people happy. It is the Holy Spirit Who helps us do what Jesus tells us to do. It is the Holy Spirit Who fills my heart with joy and peace. Sometimes He makes me feel very happy when I have done something to make people happy.

IS THE HOLY SPIRIT A DOVE?

No! The Holy Spirit is not a dove. The Holy Spirit is another name for God. The Holy Spirit is always with Jesus. He would help Jesus; He would lead Jesus; He would always be with Jesus. The Holy Spirit lives in us. He guides us and helps us love people. He helps us to make peace. That's why today people show the Holy Spirit in the form of a dove. But remember: we cannot see the Holy Spirit, but we can see the Holy Spirit at work in our lives. We often say a beautiful prayer that reminds us of the Spirit Who lives in our hearts. Listen: "Give praise to the Father Almighty, to His Son, Jesus Christ the Lord, to the Spirit Who lives in our hearts, for ever and ever. Amen." You also know another prayer: "In the name of the Father, and of the Son, and of the Holy Spirit, Amen."

WHAT IS THE LORD'S PRAYER?

The Lord's prayer is the prayer Jesus taught to His friends. Do you want to know how this happened? Jesus often liked to go to a peaceful place to speak to His Father. One day, early in the morning, Jesus' friends saw that Jesus

was already up and had left the house. They looked for Him
and found Him on a hill. He was speaking to someone whom
nobody could see. Jesus' friends wanted to be able to pray to
God in this same way. So, when Jesus came down from the
hill they asked Him: "Lord, teach us how to pray." Jesus
told them: "When you pray, pray like this:

"Our Father, who art in heaven,

hallowed be thy name,

thy Kingdom come, thy will be done on earth as it is in
heaven.

Give us this day our daily bread,

and forgive us our trespasses, as we forgive those who
trespass against us.

And lead us not into temptation, but deliver us from
evil" (Mt. 6:6-13).

We call the Our Father the Lord's Prayer because it is the
Lord Who taught it to His friends and they have taught it
to us.

WHAT DOES IT MEAN TO SAY "GIVE US THIS DAY OUR DAILY BREAD"?

We ask Our Heavenly Father that we always might
have those things we need to live and to love. We need food.
We ask God to give us life and health so that we can work to
buy food and clothing for our family. We also need love. We
ask God to open our hearts to His love so that we can always
be a happy and loving family.

WHAT ABOUT "FORGIVE US OUR TRESPASSES"?

Sometimes we do wrong. This prayer helps us to ask
God to forgive us for the times we did wrong or were for-
getful of God. We also ask God's help to help us forgive
those who hurt us in some way. It is difficult to forgive, so
we ask God's help.

WHAT ABOUT "LEAD US NOT INTO TEMPTATION"?

We ask God to keep away the spirit and the power of

evil. We ask God's help to make the good choice and keep evil away from our life.

HOW CAN GOD MAKE SOMETHING FROM NOTHING?

God can make something from nothing because He is God. That is why we say that God creates or that God is the creator of heaven and earth.

CAN MAN ALSO CREATE LIKE GOD?

No, man cannot make something from nothing. He cannot create. But God has given man a great power so that he can make many wonderful things with the things God creates. Man can transform things. He can change or transform the power of water into electricity, but it is God who has created water.

HOW CAN JESUS COME IN THE HOST?
CAN JESUS MAKE HIMSELF THAT SMALL?

Maybe there is something you forget about Jesus. You probably think that Jesus still has a body like ours, with bones and skin. The body of Christ we receive at Communion is no longer a body like the body we have. Jesus has today a new body, a risen body. The risen body of Jesus is far more beautiful and powerful than our body. With His risen body, Jesus can be everywhere and with everybody. It is because Jesus loves us that He wants to be with us and even in us. When Jesus says something about Himself, I believe what He says. I say "*Amen.*" This means, Yes, Lord, I believe Your words, because You are the Son of God and You always say the truth. At every Mass Jesus says: "Take and eat this bread for this is My body." He also says to His friends: "I am the bread of everlasting life." When I see the host and when I go to Communion the priest says: "The body of Christ." I answer: "Amen." Yes, I believe that the bread I see is the Risen Body of Jesus because He always tells the truth. Thank you Lord for staying with us. Thank you Lord for finding this way to give Your life to us.

IS IT TRUE THAT JESUS IS IN THE TABERNACLE?

Yes, we keep the bread of life in the tabernacle. Jesus says that He is the bread of life. But remember, Jesus is not there with a body that looks like our body. Jesus is there with His risen body, a very special body. Some day we shall know what it is, for we too will receive one. With His risen body, Jesus can be everywhere and with everybody. The priest keeps the bread of life in the tabernacle to bring the Lord Jesus during the week to the sick, to those who cannot come to church. During the day, many people like to come into the church to pray for a little while. They generally like to pray where we keep the bread of life. Just like God, Jesus is everywhere, but He is with us in a very special way in the bread of life.

MOMMY AND DADDY, WHY DO YOU GO TO CHURCH ON SUNDAY?

Because every Sunday God invites us to the church for the celebration of a feast. Each Sunday we meet with God and His friends in God's house. All together we like to sing to the great glory of God and we thank Him for all the gifts He shares with us. The Lord speaks to us through the Bible. We speak to Him with our prayers. The Lord also invites us to share a meal with Him and with His friends. So we, too, go up to the table of the Lord and receive the bread of life, the life of Jesus Himself. Jesus gives us His life so that when we leave the church He can be in us and give us more strength during the week to do our work with all our hearts, and to love our children and friends more and more.

WHY DO I HAVE TO BE QUIET IN THE CHURCH?

We are not always quiet in God's house. We often sing and have processions. But when we enter into a church we see that people are praying. They speak to God in the secret of their hearts. They come into the church to have a place of peace and silence to speak to God. So we don't want to disturb them. Silence and peace can be so beautiful in God's house. Sometimes we hear the priest who reads to us from the Bible. At other moments, we all stand and start singing together. Other times we listen to the beautiful organ music. Other times we make a beautiful procession. God is pleased when we do this with all our heart in the church.

WHAT IS A PRIEST?

A priest is a man whom God calls to put his life entirely at the service of God and at the service of people. Most often God asks him to take care of the people who belong to a parish.

WHAT DOES THE PRIEST DO DURING THE DAY?

The priest is the person who welcomes us into the house and family of God in the name of Jesus. It is the priest who welcomes the parents who come with their little babies to the church. Parents want their baby to enter God's family and they ask the priest to baptize their child. The priest is also the person who helps us to pray together to God when we gather in God's house on Sunday. It is the priest who reads to us the words of Jesus and helps us to understand them better. To do so he has to study a lot. When we go to Communion it is the priest who gives us Jesus, the bread of life. He also is the man who welcomes us when we come to ask God's forgiveness when we have done wrong and want to go to Confession. It is also the priest who visits those who are alone in life, those who suffer. Yes, the priest gives all his time to God and to people, just as Jesus did. It is great to be called by God to become a priest. It is beautiful for a priest to give his entire life to God and to people. We should pray often to have more priests, to have holy priests.

WHAT IS THE LITTLE RED LIGHT IN THE CHURCH?

This little red light reminds those who come into church that the Lord is there, that we can come and pray to Him.

Sometimes the red light is in a side chapel. It is there that the bread of life is kept. We call this place the chapel of the Blessed Sacrament. This chapel is beautiful, it is quiet. It is the best place to come for a little while to be with the Lord, to speak to Him in the silence of our heart.

WHY DO PEOPLE LIGHT CANDLES IN THE CHURCH?

Because people like to show their love for God, or Mary, or one of the saints whose statues we have in the church. People light the candle, they pray a little while and then they leave. But the candle will burn much longer than the time they stayed in church. It is a little like giving flowers to people we love. The flowers remind people that we love them. Even if we have to leave, the flowers remain in their house or in their room and tells them in a special way that we love them.

WHAT ARE THOSE STATUES IN THE CHURCH?

These statues are like pictures. They help us remember some of God's great friends who are already in the joy of heaven. They are already with God, they already see God. We call them the SAINTS.

ARE THERE MANY SAINTS?

Oh yes, there are hundreds, even millions of saints. You and I will be saints also, at least we hope so, for we too want to be God's friends and one day to be with Him in the joy of heaven.

WHY DO WE SAY THE SAINTS' NAMES IN PRAYERS?

We ask the saints to tell us how to live to please God. That's why we like to read or to hear about the saints. Through their life here on earth they show us things we can do to love God and to love people better. For instance, Saint Francis through his life and through the prayers he wrote, gives us a better idea of how to praise the Lord. He also shows us how we can love one another better. If we read about Saint Theresa, we learn how we can love God with all our heart.

WHO IS MARY?

Mary is a Jewish woman who lived in a small town called Nazareth. She had a very special love for God. God chose Mary and asked her to become the mother of Jesus. Mary answered "Yes" to God. Mary has always obeyed and done what God asked her to do. This is why she is the greatest of all the saints. Today she is in heaven with her son Jesus.

WHAT DID MARY DO TO BECOME A SAINT?

Mary always said "Yes" to God. She would do simple things, just like your mother, and she would do them with all her heart and love for God. When Jesus was a small child, it was Mary who taught Jesus how to eat, how to walk, how to speak. She also taught her son how to pray to God. She prepared the food for her son and took care of his clothes. When Jesus grew up, He taught Mary about His Heavenly Father. Mary kept the words of Jesus deep in her heart. She kept them and did what He said.

WHY DO WE PRAY TO MARY?
WHY DO WE HAVE HER PICTURE?

Because we, too, would like to live as she did, keeping our heart always open and willing to do the things God asks us to do. Mary can teach us and help us to always say "Yes" to God. If we follow her example we, too, will one day share her happiness and joy in heaven.

WHAT IS HEAVEN?

There is very little I know about heaven, except that I long for it with all my heart. It certainly will be the happiest and greatest surprise party we will celebrate together. Jesus tells us heaven will be like a great feast that shall never end.

He also tells us that we shall be alive, like never before, that we shall be happy like never before, and that this shall last always. In heaven, millions and millions of people will enjoy the same happiness. There shall be no tears, there shall be no wars, there shall be no pain, no death anymore. The greatest happiness about heaven is that we shall see God, our Heavenly Father, we shall be with Him, we shall also be with Jesus and the Holy Spirit. The Holy Spirit shall fill our hearts with love for everybody who will share our happiness, especially those who love us and whom we love right now, mother, father, members of the family . . . yes, we shall all love one another and be with one another for always.

WHERE IS HEAVEN?

We don't know. Maybe you think that heaven is somewhere high in the sky where we can see the moon and the stars. If you think so you are wrong. No, heaven is not somewhere in the sky where we see the planes or in the space of the astronauts. We don't know where heaven is. This is God's secret. God wants to surprise us; God wants us to put all our trust in Him. What we do know from God and from Jesus is that heaven will be full of light, full of life, full of joy, full of love and full of friends. Sometimes we hear people saying when they are very happy: this is heaven, this is paradise. What they say is true. When people are very, very happy to be together, when people love one another, when we share joy and peace, when we feel full of life, we can say that heaven starts already on earth. Can you think of a moment when you were very, very happy? . . . Maybe Christmas, maybe with your parents in your home, maybe with a friend. . . . If you can remember that joy, then you already know something of heaven. When this happens, when we are so very happy, then we don't want it to end. In heaven, our joy and our happiness will never, never end.

WHAT IS HELL?

Hell is something very sad and I certainly hope that nobody I know wants to go there! We don't know if it is a place but it certainly is a very sad situation; it is like feeling alone and lost in darkness, like having nobody who loves you. Sometimes hell starts already on earth. When in a family people hate God, when people hate one another, when people are very mean with one another, when people are wicked, then we can say: "Oh, this is like hell." Hell then is when people hate people more and more, when they destroy more and more, when they want to hate God now and for always. As you can see, it is not God who wants hell for people, but people who want hell for themselves and for others. They freely turn their back on God and on God's friends. They want nothing to do with them. They are not interested in heaven. That's hell. I do hope that nobody is interested in hell!

> *NOTE*: Heaven and hell have a great importance in the life and the imagination of young children. Even if we have tried to avoid speaking about Satan and hell, children somehow pick up stories and see pictures about both heaven and hell, angels and devils. Thus it is important to answer children's questions and to reassure the anxious child who worries about going to hell. Instead of accentuating the imagery of fire and brimstone stories we must try to remove them from the child's imagination. Therefore, we must discourage and avoid images which materialize heaven and hell and locate them in terms of space and time. Heaven or hell is less a place than a state, a life situation, a condition of man. The same is true for our risen or glorious body. Parents and teachers should discourge children who ask "how . . .". Their sole valid answer should be: "I don't know today, I shall know later." Instead, we should reorientate our answers to the "WHY". There is simultaneously a continuity and a discontinuity between our actual existence and our future existence. The Book of Revelation, chapter 21. I, states: "Then I

saw a new heaven and a new earth." But at the same time, St. Paul tells us in I Cor. 2:9: "No eye has seen, nor ear heard nor the heart of man conceived, what God has prepared for those who love Him." Therefore, let us be silent as to the "how" of this new heaven, this new creation, this new man, this new risen body. Instead, let us be strong believers in the future of mankind. Our belief rests on Jesus' promises.

WILL I GO TO HELL IF I AM NAUGHTY?

I am sure that you will not go to hell because most of the time you are a good boy (girl). Deep in your heart you love us and you love people. Deep in your heart you love God and you love Jesus. Most often you try to do what we ask you to do. You love us all. If you are naughty, this is only sometimes. You don't want to be like that always. However, when you are naughty you already know something of hell. You feel angry and sad, you feel lonely, you cut yourself off from us, you feel as if nobody loves you any more. When we are naughty God comes to our help. He calls us back. He is waiting to forgive us. God does this through your parents. We also want you back at the table, in our house, in our family. We also want to forgive you and forget about your naughtiness. What God wants for all His children is joy, peace and love. We want this also for our children. We want this for you. God does not want hell for anybody. And I know you too well. What you really want is heaven. You shall never make the wrong choice. Every day we ask God to avoid this. We say: "Deliver us from evil."

IS JUDAS IN HELL?

Nobody knows. We know that God is always willing to forgive us, even at the last moment of our life.

IS IT TRUE THAT X WILL NOT GO TO HEAVEN BECAUSE HE (OR SHE) IS NOT A CATHOLIC?

No, that's not true. First of all, God loves everybody.

He wants everybody to share with Him and with His friends the joy and the happiness of heaven. The difference between you and X is that you were born in a Catholic family. We wanted you to belong to God's family. We belong to the Catholic Church because we believe this is the church God wants us to belong to. That's why you were baptized in the Catholic Church; that's why you are a Catholic. As you became older, we told you about Jesus and about our Heavenly Father. With the love the Holy Spirit gave you, you started loving God for all He does for you. We also taught you how to speak to God, how to pray. Some of your friends were born in a Christian family but belong to a different church. Maybe they are called Episcopalians or Presbyterians. Their parents also had their children baptized in their church for they believe this is the church God wants them to belong to. They also know Jesus. They also love God, our Heavenly Father. They also receive the Holy Spirit. X . . . is not baptized. This is probably because her parents do not know Jesus. Some people even think there is no God. But God certainly loves them all. He wants them to share in the joy and the happiness of heaven. You may be sure God will find some way of bringing them into His great family. Just pray that they say "Yes" and open their hearts to the love of God when God makes Himself known to them. We can't say when this will happen, nor do we know how, but we can be sure it will happen sometime because God loves X . . . and wants her also to be happy and to belong to His great family.

ARE THERE ANGELS?

Yes, there are angels. The Bible tells us there are many, many angels. What does an angel look like? We know very little about angels because they are so different from us. They have no body, they are spirits. What we know is that they are the messengers of God, they serve God. There was the angel Gabriel who brought to Mary the message of God, that she was chosen by God to become the mother of Jesus. Angels help us at every moment. Angels are close to God and they are close to us, but that's all I know. We will have to wait until we go to heaven to know more about them.

DO THE ANGELS HAVE WINGS WITH FEATHERS?

No, angels have no bodies. Nor do they have wings and feathers. You have seen pictures where the artist drew a picture of angels with wings and feathers. The painter did this to help us understand how swift and fast the angels are to serve God. Sometimes when we are very good to people, when we say good things to a friend or to a brother or sister, when we help mother or father, then we, too, are a little like angels. We, too, are God's messengers for one another. Maybe your mother or father told you: "You are an angel, thank you!"

ARE THERE DEVILS?

Yes, there are devils. The Bible tells us that the devils are those angels who refuse to serve God. Instead of being a power of goodness like the angels, they are a power of bad. They try to get us to say "No" to God, to say "No" to people. They would like us to hate God and hate everybody. They even would like us to hate life, joy and love. When we are very naughty and wicked, we might feel the power of evil at work within ourselves. But God does not want the spirit of evil to take over. God sends us Jesus. Jesus comes to protect us from the devil. If we stay on the side of Jesus, then the devil has no power over us. Yes, Jesus is stronger than the spirit of evil. He gives us the Holy Spirit. The Spirit of love. If we follow the good ideas the Holy Spirit gives to us then we are safe.

CAN WE SEE THE DEVIL?

No, you can't see the devil. Sometimes, painters have made a picture of a devil to help us understand how wicked devils are. That's why they painted him with horns and black tail and a face that looks horrible. But devils have none of that. They have no bodies at all. They are spirits of evil and we can pray to Jesus and Mary that we never follow their wicked ideas, because they want to take us away from God.

WHY DO PEOPLE DIE?

People die for many different reasons. Usually people die after a long life. They are old. God wants us to come and live with him. Now they are ready to receive a new life that Jesus has promised to every one of us. They now deserve to enjoy forever a beautiful and peaceful life, with Jesus and with all those who are Jesus' friends. We too shall join them. We too will see God then. That shall be heaven.

WHAT HAPPENS WHEN ONE DIES?

When a person dies, Jesus tells us that we leave this life to receive a new life, a life full of joy, of light and love. We shall see God. We will meet with all of God's friends. We will join all those who love us and whom we know. Jesus tells us that we shall celebrate a feast, a joyful feast which shall never end.

WILL I ALSO DIE?

Yes, you and I will die. You and I also will receive that new life which Jesus promises to all His friends. With that new life we will be alive, we will celebrate and rejoice more than ever before. We will have many, many friends to be with, so many we won't even be able to count them.

WILL I PLAY IN HEAVEN? WILL I HAVE MY TOYS?

NOTE   When a child asks this question, he is really asking if he will be alive, if he will exist, if he will be creative. Playing represents all this for him. If we use playing in a symbolic way, we can answer the child in a positive way.

Yes, when we are with Jesus and all His friends in heaven, we will have this new life for ever. We will be happy even more than we are when we enjoy playing. Yes, we will be very happy, we will be all together, and we will know one another very well and love one another. There will be no more quarrels, no tears; but the great joy of being alive together with God, and with His friends.

DO THE DEAD SUFFER?

If someone dies after a painful sickness, he no longer suffers. He is at rest, his body can no longer suffer. Sometimes people can be so sick that those who love him ask God to call the sick person back to Him as soon as possible and give him his new life.

WHY DID GRANDFATHER DIE?

Because he was very old. His life here with us has come to an end. (or) Because he was very sick. (or) Because God found him ready now to receive a new life in heaven and join grandmother who died before him. Now they are once again together and for always.

WHY DID MY DOG (CAT) DIE?

NOTE: When children ask if their dog is in heaven, they regard the animal as a companion, a friend, and the younger the child the more he will give a "soul" and human intentions to the dog. This is due to the natural animism of children. I personally believe that it is not advisable to tell the child that the animal is alive in heaven. Our gentle negative answer to his question might not please the child; he even may reject it and continue to speak of his dog as if it were in heaven. I would not worry about this wishful behavior. Slowly he will grow and accept reality as it is. As he matures, he will be relieved to discover that his parents did not tell him something that is false.

Your dog died because he had an accident on the road. He was hit by a car. (or) Your dog was very old or he was

sick. All animals die some day; there is nothing we can do
about it.

HOW DO YOU KNOW MY DOG IS DEAD?

Because he no longer moves. His heart no longer beats.
He no longer breathes. His life has come to an end.

WHAT ARE WE GOING TO DO WITH THE DOG?

What we must do now is bury the dog or ask someone
to do it for us. We put all the things which no longer live in
the earth. Or we could burn it. We do this with dead flowers. We do this with animals also.

WHAT IS A WAKE FOR PEOPLE?

When someone dies, his family and friends come together and pray that God might give that person the new
life which Jesus promises. We say to our Heavenly Father:
"Look with favor upon Your servant, Lord, and give him
eternal life, rest and joy."

WHAT IS A FUNERAL?

A funeral is a service or a Mass which is celebrated in
the church for a person who has died. All members of his
family and his friends come together and pray for him. The
body will be blessed at the church before it is buried at the
cemetery.

WHAT IS A CEMETERY?

It is a beautiful and peaceful garden where the bodies
of those who have died are buried.

WHY ARE THE BODIES OF THOSE WHO DIE BURIED?

The bodies of those who die are buried because they
receive a new life for which they no longer need the body
they had before.

WHY DOESN'T OUR BODY GO TO HEAVEN?

Because we shall no longer need our body as we know it. God gives us a new life. He gives us a different body. We call that body a risen body or a glorious body. Just like Jesus. After His death God the Father gave Him a new life with a new risen body. Maybe you will understand better if I tell you the story of how a caterpillar becomes a butterfly. Have you ever looked at a butterfly and asked yourself where it comes from? Well, listen carefully.

The butterfly, so light, so swift, so beautiful, was first a caterpillar. A caterpillar can't do many things with its body as long as it is a caterpillar. It first is very small; then it grows and when the time has come, the caterpillar buries itself in a shell that we call a chrysalis. It looks as if the caterpillar is dead. . . . But that's not true. It is really preparing itself for a new life. One day it struggles out of the shell, out of the chrysalis, stretches its wings and there it is, no longer a caterpillar but a beautiful butterfly. Then it moves from one flower to the other flower, dancing in the air and in the wind. What happens with the old body? The old body, the chrysalis, goes back to the earth because the butterfly no longer needs it; instead, it now has a new body that is far more beautiful and can do so many more things. This story helps you to understand a little better what happens with our old body when we die. It goes back to the earth, it is buried, because we no longer need it. God gives us a new life and a new glorious body.

WHAT IS THAT NEW BODY LIKE?

We don't know. God will surprise us with it. But it will certainly be much more beautiful and powerful than the body we have now and which is already very beautiful. One day, you and I will know all this in heaven. But this will only be after we die.

WHEN WE ARE DEAD, WILL WE BE WITH DADDY AND MOMMY?

Yes, we will be with our father and mother for always,

but in a different way, in a far more beautiful way, in a very special way.

WHEN WE ARE DEAD, WILL WE BE WITH JESUS?

Yes, Jesus is already with you today, but you can't see Him and often you forget that your great friend is with you because you don't pay enough attention to Him. But when we receive our new life, we will be with Jesus in a very special way. We will see Him. Jesus will be in us and with us for always. Jesus tells us it will be much better than the life we have today.

WHY DO PEOPLE CRY WHEN SOMEONE DIES IN THE FAMILY?

Because those who remain on earth will no longer see the person who died until they are once again together in the joy of heaven. This is hard for people who have lived together many years and who have loved one another very much. They are so used to one another. It is very hard for the person who remains alive. Imagine someone you love very much and live with in a happy home leaving for a very, very long trip, a trip that lasts many years. You certainly would miss him very, very much. The day he leaves, maybe you too would cry.

Maybe people are sad because they think more of themselves. If they knew more about the new life God gives to the person who dies, if they knew more about his happiness and peace, they would not be so sad. I know a wonderful grandmother and grandfather who had been very happy together for many, many years. They had many children and grandchildren. When the grandfather died, this is what the grandmother said to her children and grandchildren who were so sorry for her and for themselves. She said: "Children, we should not cry. God gave me a good husband. He has been a wonderful father and grandfather. We have lived together more than forty years. I thank God for the wonderful life we have had together. Today I thank God for the new and happy life God gives to grandfather. Someday, God will call me also, and you, too. In heaven, our big family will once again be gathered, we will love one another even more than we could love one another here on earth. In heaven, there will be no end to our life and to our happiness. Let us ask grandfather to help us love one another so that some day we all will see one another again in heaven." This grandmother did not cry the day her husband died. Because she knew her husband was alive with God and also with us. She knew that grandfather was now, more than ever before, taking care of all his children and grandchildren.

Even if she no longer sees grandfather, she knows that grandfather is very close to her and to his family. Even today, when her grandchildren tell her of good report cards at school, or of something good they did to help their mother or father, the grandmother tells them: "I am proud of you and very happy. I am sure grandfather feels as I do. He also is very happy with you and with the good job you have done. . . ." Rather than cry, this grandmother always has kept a peaceful heart and a loving smile. Maybe it is because she is never sorry for herself. She never thinks of herself but instead she rejoices and thanks the Lord for the new and happy life her husband is enjoying now that he is in a new, special way with God and with all of us forever and ever.